To Steve

Hope all ~~~~~~~~~~.

Dreams Really Do Come True!

Best wishes,

Coach Jim Johnson

STEVE-

AS A FELLOW ARCADIA ALUM ('78)
IT'S AN HONOR TO SHARE THIS BOOK
WITH YOU!

GOD BLESS ALWAYS,

MIKE LATONA

M000076975

26 June 2011
Methodist Somers Church

"*From the man behind Jason McElwain's success comes the play-book behind the headlines. But this is not a manual for the makings of a great game; it is a workbook for the makings of a great person. Coach Johnson explores the years, weeks and days of "coaching" moments that led up to that unforgettable game, and each chapter is punctuated by reflective questions that will challenge pro and bench-warmer alike. Inspirational and thought-provoking, this book is a must-read for young athletes, coaches or anyone just looking for a rebound.*"

—Steve Hartman, CBS News correspondent

"*This story is truly inspirational. You will be touched by the warmth of a caring high school coach. It is awesome baby!*"

—Dick Vitale, ESPN basketball analyst

"*Jim's and Jason's story is one of the most inspirational achievements I have EVER seen in sport. They capture the very essence of sport—the joy, the purity, the passion of competing. With this book we have the chance to be reminded how lucky we are—and why we play the game.*"

—Jim Nantz, CBS sportscaster

"*I find in case after case after case, there is a person who sees the talent and passion and that's what attracts them. And that's what [Coach Johnson] did. When you look at people on the autism spectrum, there is a mentor involved.*"

—Temple Grandin, author, speaker and autism activist

"*A high-school coach, much more than in the pros, has the opportunity to touch lives in numerous ways. Jim Johnson demonstrated that marvelously when he put his autistic team manager into a game. What resulted makes you believe more strongly in the human spirit; that there's some greater being out there than human. This book is a must-read for people who believe in miracles or need to believe in them.*"

—Jeff Van Gundy, NBA head coach and sportscaster

"Jim Johnson vividly captures a compelling basketball season that goes far beyond an autistic boy's night in the spotlight. This high-school coach offers important reflections—for people at all levels of athletics—about what's really important in life. An excellent read."

—Pat Williams, senior vice president, Orlando Magic; motivational speaker and author

"That relationship between J-Mac and Coach Johnson was pure and innocent, for all the right reasons. No one told him, 'You spend a lot of time with this kid, you're going to get a lot of publicity.' Coach Johnson was just hoping to get him in a game. God looked at that; he blessed that decision and he allowed the world to see it."

—Billy Donovan, University of Florida head basketball coach

"I think it's a tremendous accomplishment and a great lesson, a reminder that a community needs to give these people all the opportunities it can. It doesn't matter whether your IQ is 20 or 200. Everybody has a gift inside of them, and it's up to the community to unlock that gift."

—Dr. Timothy Shriver, chair, International Special Olympics

"What a great and neat thing Coach Johnson did, giving J-Mac that opportunity. It made all the difference in the world. You do the right thing like that, you may change a life forever. It had an impact across the board."

—John Calipari, University of Kentucky head basketball coach

"The great lesson here for a coach, parent, teacher, uncle, or grandmother is in believing in young people—to have that belief that young people have more in them than we can ever estimate. The decision that night is the culmination of Coach Johnson's belief in J-Mac for years."

—Tom Rinaldi, ESPN reporter

"I've known from the first day of coaching with Jim in Rochester, he's one of those guys I labeled as 'he just gets it.' We all have an opportunity to affect a lot of lives, and that's what he does."

—Jay Wright, Villanova University head basketball coach

A COACH
and a
MIRACLE

Life Lessons From a Man Who
Believed in an Autistic Boy

A Coach *and a* Miracle

Copyright © 2011
by Jim Johnson and Mike Latona.

All rights reserved.
Printed in the United States of America.
No part of this book may be used or reproduced
in any manner whatsoever without permission
except in the case of brief quotations embodied
in critical articles or reviews.

Cover Design: James Arneson Art & Design (Jaad)
Concept: Linda Rivers
Interior Design: James Arneson Art & Design (Jaad)

A COACH
and a
MIRACLE

Life Lessons From a Man Who
Believed in an Autistic Boy

JIM JOHNSON
with
Mike Latona

Contents

Dedication

To my wife, Pat; and son, Tyler.
Thanks for all your love and support. Life has been wonderful
because I have both of you.

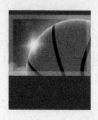

Foreword

MANY OF US CONNECTED WITH UNIVERSITY OF Florida basketball first heard of Jason McElwain just days before we made the NCAA Final Four, in late March 2006. Once the guys saw the game video, they were all talking about it. Everybody was touched by the story; it was just incredible. By the time we traveled to the Final Four, all of our guys knew who J-Mac was.

Not long after we got to Indianapolis for the Final Four, I received a phone call from our sports information director saying that J-Mac was being honored that weekend by appearing at all the shoot-arounds so he could meet the players. We were at Butler University the day before our semifinal game against George Mason, and I thought it would be a great experience for our kids to see J-Mac in person. Unfortunately for him, his dad, and Coach Johnson, they got caught in traffic and couldn't make it. But later we were having a team meal and I was told, "Listen, they're over here staying at the same hotel—can they come by?" I said, "Sure."

The funniest thing was J-Mac going around saying, "Where's [Joakim] Noah, where's Noah? I want to meet Noah." The players let him pull up a chair and took some pictures with him. He was saying, "You better watch out for Glen Davis," referring to LSU's star, "Big Baby" Davis.

J-Mac is outspoken, in a good way. It was great for me to take a step back and watch our team interact with him, and him with them. I hope our guys made him feel like a million dollars. I was honored to spend that time with Coach Johnson as well, based on the pivotal role he had played in Jason's ascent to sudden stardom.

We went on to beat George Mason and UCLA for the first of our two straight national championships. I really believe that Jason and Coach Johnson were a blessing for us that year. They helped us understand that with our team on the national stage, we have the opportunity to inspire others. By looking at this young man and what he accomplished, we were energized and motivated to play the game the way it's supposed to be played. We played terrific team basketball both years that we won the NCAAs. Even at the major collegiate level, you need to try and keep it innocent and pure. We've had a lot of success at Florida, but the minute you start getting out of that team focus—being selfish, looking out just for yourself—it becomes very, very difficult.

I remember getting goose bumps the first time I saw the J-Mac video—all the scoring he did, his teammates constantly passing the ball, the crowd going crazy. When you look at all the seemingly insurmountable odds J-Mac overcame, you couldn't have scripted it better. It makes you think of all the other kids who are the fifteenth, sixteenth man on their team.

A team is not just the Joakim Noahs and the Al Horfords, guys who starred for my national championship teams in 2006 and 2007. It takes a special kid to be the fifteenth or sixteenth person. He knows that his playing time will be limited or even nonexistent, but he makes just as strong a commitment to the program as everyone else. That in turn promotes team unity, right on up to the starters.

When Jason did get a chance to play, it was like the *Rudy* story, a chance to fulfill his dream. Daniel E. "Rudy" Ruettiger made just one tackle, which may seem insignificant to some people. But it was huge for Rudy, because that tackle meant everything he had worked for. It was the same with J-Mac. Because of the time he had put in, just the fact that he was playing in a game made it a moment he'd remember for a long, long time. J-Mac is an inspiration to all of us, because despite the daily challenges in his life, he had a great, innocent belief in the game of basketball, in his team, and in his coach.

And Jim Johnson wanted to reach out to him. I look at how Coach went out of his way to make sure that J-Mac had an unbelievable high school experience, to give him that opportunity. Their relationship was genuine; it was not built on one taking from the other or trying to benefit from the other for any personal gain.

This story must have made Jim break down and cry as a coach, knowing that he had made a dream come true for one of his players. It also appeals deeply to the rest of us coaches, at all levels, who dedicate ourselves to bettering the lives of young men and women. You could coach a lifetime and not experience something this heartfelt, even though you hope every single year that you will.

For five minutes that night, you saw put into a capsule what coaching is all about. To me, this is much bigger than winning and losing; it's about human life. There's so much here to inspire other people. What happened was a blessing. Look at all the other lives that were touched. There are so many teaching tools that came out of that game in Rochester.

A Coach and a Miracle

Often in the coaching profession it's perceived that if you win, you're great; if you lose, you're bad. You feel that if you don't win enough, you're probably not going to have a job for very long. So it's easy to lose sight of what's important, and you have to bring yourself back to that all the time.

Jim helped bring coaches back to their mission. Everything he did with J-Mac was for the right reasons. Here's a young kid in the last game of the year, just the people in his hometown watching him, no national TV attention just yet. It didn't matter that he wasn't part of a national championship team. It was his championship.

To me, the wins and losses will come and go. But a story like this can carry on through the years. People look at how our Gators won back-to-back national titles and predict that we'll go down as one of the greatest teams ever. But twenty-five or thirty years from now, I don't know how vivid our accomplishments will be in people's minds outside of Florida. The story of J-Mac and Coach Johnson, on the other hand, is something that will stick with people everywhere. And because of the Internet, you can show what happened over and over. I don't know if anything else will ever equal that.

You can never underestimate the possibility that when you're passionate about something, God has a chance to use you in a way that inspires other people. There are things that happen spiritually that we're not capable of applying ourselves. I never thought I'd get to play for Providence and go to the Final Four, get drafted in the NBA, coach at Florida, and win back-to-back national championships. I'm not capable of that on my own. It's the blessings of God.

God works through all of us in different ways and can touch us in different ways. When you look at the spiritual side of what happened with J-Mac and Coach Johnson, I really think something was there. There's no question that the hand of God was in all this. Jim's motives involving his team manager were pure—no one told him, "If you spend a lot of time with this kid, you're going to get a lot of publicity." He was just hoping to get J-Mac into a game.

God looked at that, he blessed that decision, and he allowed the world to see it. What happened one night in Rochester, New York, was beyond anything human.

Billy Donovan
Head men's basketball coach
University of Florida
NCAA champions, 2006 and 2007

one

Define Your Passion

What do you really want to do in life? What burns way down inside of you? What do you absolutely love to do?

VIRTUALLY ALL THE STUDENTS IN THE PACKED bleachers across from me rose to their feet, cheering wildly and jumping up and down. All I could do was sit down and cry.

Never before had I made a coaching move with this kind of impact. Never in my career had I felt such emotion. You'd think we had just won a championship. It wasn't a buzzer-beating basket; it wasn't a heave from half-court that made the place go nuts. In fact, it wasn't even a play. All I had done was turn toward the player with uniform number 52, point my index finger at him, and say, "J-Mac."

Up bounced seventeen-year-old Jason McElwain. My team manager's dream finally came true on February 15, 2006, the last home game of his senior year. Jason—or J-Mac, a tag I had hung on him early in his sophomore year—was about to see his first varsity action.

He was small and skinny, standing all of five feet seven inches and weighing only 120 pounds, and his blond hair was partially covered by a headband. You may wonder just why the fans were going so nuts.

Because Jason was not your average team manager. He's also autistic and learning-disabled.

He had been cut three straight years from his teams, the last two from the varsity by me. But he lives and breathes basketball, and was so dedicated that I had planned for months to give him a special treat on Senior Night: getting him a uniform and hopefully finding him some playing time as well.

Jason had taken a lot of grief over the years because of his disability. Go to just about any high school, and the kid who's a little different gets singled out for ridicule. In Jason's case, he was an easy target with his unusually loud voice, his tendency to laugh at inappropriate times, and his habit of repeating things he heard other people say. Occasionally I would say something to the team and Jason would repeat it several times—never anything very insightful; just general comments like "We gotta play as hard as we can," and those kinds of things.

Basketball was his salvation, a constant bright light that outshone the teasing in the hallways. It kept him enthusiastic and filled his mind with pleasant thoughts. He was a bona fide hoops junkie—loved watching the game on television, loved Kobe Bryant, memorized Final Four rosters, scouted our high school opponents, you name it.

Above all, he burned with passion for Greece Athena, the high school for which I'm head coach and he proudly served as team manager. Jason had an infectious attitude that was so positive. I saw how, gradually, the kids on the team started to develop an appreciation for what he brought to the table every day. In the words of Ralph Waldo Emerson, "Nothing great was ever achieved without enthusiasm." That's a terrific life lesson.

Jason was almost fanatical in his devotion. I doubt there was a comparable team manager in all of Rochester, all of New York, all of anywhere. On game days he would go up to the black-board at the beginning of each class and write "Beat Arcadia" or whomever we were playing that night. The players came to greatly respect him because he cared so deeply and wanted so badly to contribute. As much as some of his autistic habits and mannerisms would drive the guys nuts, he was one of us.

If there's one thing that will forever link me with Jason, it's our love of basketball. I've coached for thirty years and I am thoroughly happy with the life I've chosen. Coaching gets into your blood. You aren't getting paid much for doing it, or maybe not getting paid at all, but you love the challenges, the chance to get to a higher level, being in the gym working with kids, teaching basketball. The game has burned way down inside me since I was a little kid, so Jason's passion feeds right into mine.

Jason had persevered and worked hard on his basketball skills, and yet I had to cut him from varsity his junior and senior seasons—an obvious yet difficult decision. But at the beginning of 2005–06, I promised him the uniform for Senior Night and also ventured the possibility of his seeing some playing time. As the season rolled on, Jason checked in regularly about the uniform's status. I said I was working on it, but the truth is I had much bigger issues at hand—in many respects the biggest problems of my career.

Our talented team had been torn by internal strife involving some players' parents. They had demanded that I remove my long-time assistant coach because he now had two sons on the team, and the parents perceived favoritism by the coaching staff concerning those boys' playing time. The attack on my personal integrity cut so deeply that I seriously considered stepping down as head coach just as the season was beginning. I searched my soul as never before, staying on only after my wife, colleagues, and friends noted that I should heed the same advice I'm always dispensing to my players about persevering through tough situations.

Sometimes you've got to simply put your trust in God, because you can't figure out why certain things happen. Through good times and bad, I feel that God is there for me whether he's providing comfort or trying to challenge me to become a better person. Boy, was he challenging me in 2005–06. Had it not been for my faith, family, and friends, Lord knows where I would have been on February 15. All I know is that it wouldn't have been on the Athena bench.

Our team stumbled out of the gate during the season's first half, barely playing .500 ball, before our collective perseverance began to pay off. We came into Senior Night having won eight out of nine games, and actually had a chance to tie for the league title.

I held firm on my promise to Jason, making the necessary arrangements to activate him for the game against Spencerport. Senior Night is always a special time, when we introduce the seniors and their parents prior to the varsity game. The seniors were introduced alphabetically and Jason got a large ovation. We always include our team managers in Senior Night, but Jason was the first manager ever to don a uniform. All the early-season troubles were forgotten in the festive atmosphere surrounding J-Mac's varsity debut.

He had waited for that night in the same way people wait for their graduation, for their wedding day—a moment so monumental, it seems like it's never going to arrive. For years Jason had emphasized that he was on the Athena team, and the classmates who enjoyed taking the air out of his balloon would remind him he was just the manager/water boy. Here was one night I had made sure they couldn't say that.

During the warm-ups Jason hoisted up nothing but his specialty, three-point shots. Some went in and some didn't, but it didn't really matter. He was launching those shots alongside his teammates, in front of the fans. He was *on the team*.

Not long after the opening tip, chants of "J-Mac" began floating down from our cheering section known as "the Sixth Man." Obviously, simply seeing J-Mac dressed for the game but not playing wasn't going to work for them.

Chances had seemed good for him to get some action, since we were playing the last-place team in our Monroe County Division II league. We had just whipped Spencerport 67-54 a month earlier, at their place.

But I was frustrated in the first half of our rematch because we didn't get that lead quite up to where I felt comfortable putting J-Mac in, and I was also still trying to give all the other subs sufficient playing time. We led 16-8 after one quarter and 28-15 at halftime, but I needed the point spread to be wider. Once I put Jason in the game, I wanted to leave him there until the end. Not that I thought we were going to blow the lead because of him, but I really wanted to let him finish so that he would have a reasonable chance of scoring a basket. To have him make a token appearance for one possession would have insulted his dignity. In fact, I wanted everything about his appearance on the court to look as natural as possible.

If he could score even once, wow, what a great layer of elation that would add. Hopefully it would turn out just like two years earlier, when he played in the junior varsity's final home game thanks to a kind gesture by that team's coach, Jeff Amoroso. Jason didn't score a basket that night, but he was fouled on a three-point attempt and made all three of his free throws.

Although I didn't observe unusual body language from J-Mac on February 15, I did notice that he departed from his customary manager's role of running down to the end of the bench and getting water for the players. This time I don't think he wanted me to forget about him, so he hung right next to me the whole time. Being that we had no substitute team manager, it was self-service for water that night. I'm very sure all he could think was, "When's Coach going to get me in?"

Other players might be offended or embarrassed by being inserted into the game when the outcome has already been decided, but this would mean the world to J-Mac. He just wanted to get out on that floor once and show his stuff to the crowd.

We opened a twenty-six-point lead, 50-24, by the end of the third quarter, and I still hadn't gotten Jason on the floor. I think the entire Athena section was getting ready to throttle me if I didn't put him in soon; they had been chanting "J-Mac" since the game began and were getting more insistent with every minute that passed.

Finally, there was a stoppage in play with just over four minutes remaining and I thought, "The time is right now." I got up and gestured to Jason; Rob Zappia, a teammate, slapped him on the back; I gave him a pat on the backside as he sprinted by; and my assistant coach, Mike Setzer, gave him a high ten. All the other players started clapping for him.

J-Mac was so eager to go in, he almost didn't check in. For all his dreaming about this moment coming to fruition, he actually seemed a bit like a fish out of water now that it had arrived—as if he were thinking, "What's going on here?" He had to be redirected to the scorers' table. Then came the booming voice of our public-address announcer, Jason Bunting: "Number fifty-two, Jason McElwain!"

These extra few seconds gave me some time to pick up on an amazing gesture unfolding in the student section. Not only were the fans cheering at the top of their lungs; they were also furiously waving dozens of placards with blow-up photos of J-Mac. A player's dad, Jay Shelofsky, had taken some pictures of Jason earlier in the season and then had his face enlarged and attached to wooden sticks. The Sixth Man had kept the placards hidden all night, and weren't going to raise them until Jason was in the game. Some students were also holding oversize letters and forming a row to spell J-M-A-C.

Zappia and another Athena player, Rickey Wallace, pointed at this massive display of support and started jumping up and down. If you were the opposition, you probably didn't know what to make of this—a simple, ordinary substitution is made and the crowd and players go absolutely berserk?

All of this occurred in just a few seconds' time, and I was simply in a state of shock, slumped down on my seat. Mike Setzer came over and asked if I was OK, and I said I was.

It was a huge sense of relief to get Jason in. Regardless of whether he scored, he was guaranteed celebrity status around school the next day, simply by the fact that he had seen action.

Play resumed, and Jason's varsity career was officially under way as the crowd continued to buzz. Our substitute guard, Terrance McCutchen, brought the ball up-court and passed inside to our substitute center, Brian Benson, who immediately kicked it out to J-Mac in the right corner and set a screen for him. Everybody rose in anticipation and shrieked as J-Mac launched his first attempt with 3:45 left in the game.

Air ball.

It was on line, but clear over the rim. I think he was all pumped up and just let it fly with a little extra juice. The crowd went quiet for a second, then began buzzing again. Some fans might be tempted to derisively chant "air ball" after a shot like that, but these people wanted so badly for Jason to have some success.

Spencerport grabbed J-Mac's missed shot, went down-court, and missed as well. Benson latched on the loose ball, started a fast break, and then dished ahead to J-Mac, who dribbled left-handed to the hoop and took a pretty-looking runner with 3:29 to go.

Off the rim.

More shrieks were followed by groans. All I could do was put my head in my hands. My decision to play Jason may have been an immense crowd pleaser, but the last thing I wanted was for him to have a negative legacy, for people to be saying years later,

"Hey, remember when J-Mac came in and shot all those air balls? Jeez, Jason couldn't hit the broad side of a barn."

We're told that we can't pray in public schools, but that didn't stop me from saying, "Please, God, let him make just one basket," after he missed the first one. Following the missed layup, I started praying harder.

Fortunately, God must be a basketball fan. He had a message to deliver to the rest of the world—in my opinion, nothing short of a miracle.

ACTION STEP: *Write down the things you love to do. Think back to when you were a child—what were the activities you loved to do then? Pick one or two that you could pursue now, and list how you could do them as a hobby or, better yet, make them part of your occupation. The more I've studied people who have followed their dream and passion, the more I've seen how living that way on a daily basis makes life more exciting. In exit interviews with my senior players, I used to encourage them to pursue careers in which the job market had the best openings. Now I encourage them to follow their passion. When you do that, the money tends to find you.*

two

Define Your Mission

How can you use your passion in a positive way? How can you raise your sense of self-worth and accomplishment, and leave this world a better place? What did God put you on this earth to do?

COACHING WASN'T THE PATH I HAD EXPECTED TO follow in order to maintain my passion for basketball. Although I played and enjoyed a bunch of sports growing up in the 1960s and '70s, my ultimate dream was to be a pro basketball player. I was a three-year varsity guard at Greece Arcadia High School, only a couple of miles from Athena, playing under my dad, Gene Johnson. As a senior in 1976–77 I was voted team MVP and named All-Monroe County.

In college I didn't play past my sophomore year, so when I saw that my dream of playing in the pros wasn't in the cards, I really wanted to stay involved as a coach. In retrospect, my coaching tendencies were there from an early age. I'm the oldest of six children and as a kid I was always an organizer and leader, making up baseball and basketball tournaments in my neighborhood. I'd even make up rules for games of stickball.

I've never regretted my career choice. Even when I go through rough patches, I ask myself, "But if I don't coach, what could I do that's half as exciting?" Nothing can top the feeling of being in a packed high school gymnasium on a Friday night. It's an awesome atmosphere, full of electricity. I remember that it got so loud in our cozy gym during my years at Greece Olympia, I couldn't hear myself think. I thought I was going to go deaf during some close games. It felt like it was 110 degrees, and I sweat through everything. My wife told me I couldn't wear a suit there anymore.

I began coaching right out of college. At one time I had the chance to pursue a full-time coaching career at the collegiate level, which potentially offered more money and prestige. But I felt my mission was to teach and coach in my hometown of Greece, planting roots in the same school district where I grew up.

You get such highs working with kids, seeing them mature. It's true that coaches at every level are judged by wins and losses, but personal development at the scholastic level means so much.

I've taught physical education for as long as I've coached. I've always been a mover, somebody who likes to go out and enjoy different activities, so teaching phys ed was a way I could keep that part of my life. Sitting behind a desk was never for me.

As a teacher you have to learn how to deal with different personalities. Some kids love to come to phys ed; others don't enjoy it and you're trying to find ways to reach them. They're mortified about their physical appearance, perhaps, and don't want to change into shorts. You try to talk to them individually and find out what they're all about. The more they realize that you care about them, the more motivation they find.

Then again, most times a phys ed teacher only sees students in one-hour blocks. Coaching is vital for me because I get to form much deeper bonds and thus make a greater impact. In basketball you're with your athletes six days a week, occasionally seven, for a period of four months. Plus, a basketball roster is fairly small, so you get a chance to have much closer relationships with players than in football, for instance.

Different coaches have different ways of succeeding, yet I feel the core values have to be there regardless of your approach. Bobby Knight and Tony Dungy might use different language and decibel levels, but the intangibles they impress on their teams are vital—the need to be on time, always seeking to improve, caring for each other. I remember going to a clinic by Duke University's Mike Krzyzewski, and how he emphasized that the bottom line in coaching is relationships. That reminds me of a little quote I've heard over the years: "It's not about the X's and O's; it's about the Johnnys and Joes."

The late John Wooden is probably my earliest coaching role model, somebody who showed that there's still room for integrity in coaching even when you've made it big. I used to beg my parents to let me stay up on Saturday nights to watch his great UCLA teams play, back in the late 1960s and early '70s, when college basketball wasn't as popular on television. As I grew older I came to greatly respect Coach Wooden for his many wisdom-filled sayings, such as "Make each day your masterpiece," and "When you're through learning, you're through."

People like John Wooden, Tony Dungy, and Dean Smith have shown a real passion for what they do while also maintaining high integrity, trustworthiness, and honesty. It seems that everything they've touched has turned to gold instead of garbage; every person and situation around them got better. On the other hand, every now and then you hear of highly successful coaches who put their jobs and their schools in tough spots due to some sort of NCAA violation or personal scandal. So, you can't just preach integrity; you've got to live it.

My approach to coaching in recent years has fallen along the lines of Coach Dungy's—showing a bit of a softer side and doing a better job of showing that I care. I don't yell as much as I used to, and am not as animated in game situations. I have so much respect for the way Coach Dungy has handled himself in a first-class manner. He doesn't lose his cool very often, and gets his point across without a lot of the extras.

I've worked hard to improve myself by reading books by famous coaches and personal-success gurus, attending coaches' camps and clinics, and sending letters to successful coaches to pick their brains. I want to find out what works for them. Quite a few years ago I wrote to John Calipari, who has gone to the Final Four with both the University of Massachusetts (1996) and the University of Memphis (2008), and I asked for some advice. He actually called me up and spent a few minutes talking to me, not even knowing who I was, and was very gracious. For him to pick up the phone out of the blue—that's something I'll never forget.

Though I have immense respect for all these coaches, and am friends with many who have made it big, I'm not a disciple of any one coach. When you're not yourself, players can tell that you're trying to hide behind being a Bobby Knight or a Tony Dungy. You've got to try and pick the approach that fits your personality.

In case you couldn't tell, I'm a fairly driven person. I'm constantly looking to improve myself and my players, continually trying to raise my standards. On many mornings I'll listen to some kind of motivational or educational tape while getting ready for work. Some would say I'm a bit quirky in my thirst for knowledge: George Giordano, a colleague from Greece Olympia, used to kid me because I'd write down my goals and then tape them all over the wall.

A few years back I began making more of a concerted effort to pass values on to my players, to give them something beyond just basketball. I started by instituting a weekly "life lesson." It was a concept I picked up from Tom Osborne, the great University of Nebraska football coach, from his autobiography, *Faith in the Game*. I've accumulated a big notebook full of potential themes from books, newspapers, and sports magazines. I'm always looking for something that links teamwork, work ethic, attitude, and enthusiasm.

Once a week I pick a theme pertinent to what I'm trying to get across at that time. If the emphasis is on team, I might highlight "There is no *I* in *team*," "Teamwork makes the dream work," and "The word *TEAM* stands for Together Everyone Accomplishes More." If I'm emphasizing work ethic, I can pull out "The harder I work, the luckier I get." Some of my themes during the 2005–06 season were integrity and honesty, for which I used Oprah Winfrey's "Real integrity is doing the right thing knowing that nobody's going to know whether you did it or not."

Admittedly, there were probably lots of times my message was too heavy for players who simply wanted to play hoops.

"As a seventeen-year-old, sometimes it was hard to grasp. That's like reading the Bible. You read the words, but you might not really understand it until later," said Rickey Wallace, a forward and senior tri-captain on the 2005–06 squad.

"When you're that age, the stuff doesn't make sense; all you want to do is get done with practice. But the older you get, you realize those were good lessons Coach taught us," said Terrance McCutchen, a junior guard that year.

The one thing that has absolutely struck me over and over about Jim, he's just a deeply humble guy. He doesn't see himself as the master, the controller, the person who has to be turning people into chess pieces. He understands that "team" is a teaching opportunity. Unfortunately there are coaches who lose that humility in the glare of winning and losing. They see wins and losses as the acumen of their ability and skill.

—Tom Rinaldi, ESPN reporter

A vital link I have to Tom Osborne, Dean Smith, and Tony Dungy—all devout Christians—is my strong Catholic faith. I've always been a practicing Catholic, but I feel I've experienced a rejuvenation the past six or seven years, going through a prayer ritual every morning and overall feeling much closer to God.

I'm always looking for guidance from God, and it's important to have trust, because sometimes you can't figure out why certain things happen to you. I do feel that God is there for me, but he also challenges me to become a better person. I'm a big believer that God creates a world that's both challenging and exciting.

My religious beliefs help keep me centered on the importance of being a role model. On the one hand, my public school setting prevents me from anything resembling the preaching of religion. Unfortunately, in this politically correct day and age, you have to be careful or you could even lose your job. It's very tricky.

On the other hand, I can certainly reflect the goodness of God by living out my principles. Some of my players are Catholic and they see me at Mass. I may not spend all day talking about my faith, but the team knows I attend church, am loyal to my wife and child, and maintain a drug-free and smoke-free lifestyle.

Hopefully my actions will encourage players to place more emphasis on their own spiritual lives. High school can involve a ton of trials and tribulations, and having that spiritual foundation is a huge help when things aren't going so well.

For many years I've had a plaque hanging on the wall of my home office. It sums up a lot of where I'm at in my coaching life and faith life. It's called the Coach's Prayer and its author is unknown. It reminds me to ask God for the abilities that count the most: building character and self-esteem, keeping an even temper, treating everybody with respect regardless of ability, being patient. It closes with "Lord, whether we may win or lose / May all who are watching see / The kind of coach at every game / That you would have me be."

There's a picture on my wall right next to that plaque; it illustrates one of the reasons I need to keep reciting the prayer. It shows me stomping my foot on the sideline floor in frustration, arms raised and hair flying every which way, during a Section 5 playoff game while I was coaching Greece Olympia.

Those things don't happen during games quite as much now. If I'm calm in a tight situation, then so are my players. I've always been a high-energy coach, which I think is fine because you want high energy out of your team as well. But I think I've evolved more into the approach exhibited by my father while he was my varsity coach at Greece Arcadia. He believed in yelling less so as to better get people's attention when he did yell. Otherwise you might as well get used to being tuned out.

I've also toned down during practice. I used to yell a lot— not necessarily in a negative sense, but I'd constantly be stopping practice to point something out. Now I let the kids play more and keep practice at a pretty quick pace, because that's how the game is played. You don't stop after every transition.

I can still get after the players pretty well, but I think it has a stronger effect if I don't do it all the time. I like to bust chops during practice, and that's another evolution, because I've always been pretty intense. But it's not all life or death. The kids like having fun, and so do I. I've also gotten better at catching kids doing things right, not just pointing out the negatives.

I try to uphold a family atmosphere on the team, being approachable and making all the kids, as well as their parents, feel included. We spend a lot of time off the court during the season, having regular pasta dinners and other social events. I send every kid in my program a birthday card and have their birthdays marked down in my datebook. As a coach and leader you're building a family, and it always means a lot to me when I get a nice note of thanks from a player at the end of a season, or get invited to a graduation party.

These family ideals unquestionably stem from my dad, Gene, and my mom, Rita. Both my parents are retired teachers and have always modeled how to treat people right—all kinds of people, whether they're athletes, special-needs kids like J-Mac, or folks you meet on the street. Much as I'd like to think I'm my own person, I'm very proud of the fact that I've taken on the same career as my parents and become a high school coach in Greece, just like my dad. We stay in close touch. My parents come to my games and we often sit together during Mass at my childhood parish, Our Mother of Sorrows, just like we did every Sunday when I was a kid.

My wife, Pat, whom I married in 1982, and our only child, Tyler, who was born in 1990, have strengthened that family infrastructure. I try not to take Pat and Tyler for granted, considering that so many of my players have come from split households and carry all kinds of baggage as a result. Pat and Tyler have always been very supportive of what I do for a living, which is no small gesture—coaching is an extremely time-consuming profession. God and family should always be your highest priorities, but sometimes the priorities can get out of whack. Many coaches fall victim to overlaps with their full-time jobs, faith, and family due to hours and hours spent at practice, at summer camps, and on buses. And there's not a whole lot extra in your paycheck to reflect that commitment.

Sure, there's glamour in what we do too. We run the practices, we patrol the sidelines, and we're the ones who get quoted in the newspaper. And if everything falls into place, you get some wins and the adulation that comes with that success. I had nothing to be ashamed of in that respect, having come into the 2005–06 season with 233 career wins, mostly at Greece Olympia and then Greece Athena where I've coached since 1996.

Yet what's been even more satisfying for me has been seeing young men go on to succeed as adults. I feel just like a proud father. Two of my high school players have gone on to Division I colleges: Demond Stewart, from Greece Olympia, who became a high-scoring guard at Niagara University and was named Metro Atlantic Athletic Conference Player of the Year in 2000–01; and Brian Benson, my center from Greece Athena who earned a full ride to the University of New Hampshire beginning in 2008. I've also had lots of players who have competed at the Division III level.

Equally significant are my former athletes who have found success in areas other than basketball. One of my Olympia players, Alex Okosi, was a Nigerian student. He had no family in the area, and my own aunt took him in for a few years. Alex has now become a top executive for MTV Africa, and in 2007 he was the cover story subject for *Forbes* magazine.

Meanwhile, Olympia's Anibal Soler is an administrator in the Rochester City School District, and Mike Grosodonia, also from Olympia, is the head basketball coach at Aquinas Institute, having taken over for my good friend Mike Dianetti, who died of cancer in the spring of 2007. It's a joy when you see the people from your basketball family go on to succeed in the biggest game, the game of life.

As a pro coach, it's about doing what is needed to win the game. But in high school, somebody like Jim has more of a responsibility to teach so many more things.

—Jeff Van Gundy, former head coach of the NBA's New York Knicks and Houston Rockets, now a prominent NBA broadcaster

---

Amid these success stories, I'd like to think I can empathize with players of all skill levels—mainly because I've covered that entire spectrum as a player. Although basketball emerged as my main sport, the game did not come easily to me. I was a scrub in middle school before becoming a first-team all-county point guard in high school. But then I was cut as a sophomore at the State University of New York at Cortland, never to play organized ball again.

I don't think all people realize what coaching, particularly high school coaching, is about. At that level it isn't just wins and losses, [or] what was your record last year. If a coach is taking his job seriously, he is advancing the human race.

—Reggie Witherspoon, head basketball coach, University at Buffalo

---

Being cut was shocking for me, and I still don't think it should have happened, but the bottom line is that it *did* happen. You get a lot of life lessons by playing on sports teams, and one of them is humility. You may have grown up a star, and now suddenly you're on the bench. So I can fully relate to the experience of guys who see their dreams squashed when I have to cut or bench them.

✳

That brings me back to Mr. Jason McElwain. Perhaps not every adult instructor or coach has the patience for reaching out to an autistic person. But if I'm really true to my mission, then I'm going to make time for a young man like Jason.

I first got to know J-Mac during his sophomore year, in 2003. *Scrawny* is the first word that comes to mind in describing him: small and thin, especially compared with the other players.

But basketball was his number one passion, and that's what brought him to tryouts. My first impression of him was that he was a little guy with this very deep, loud voice—no match for his outward appearance. You'd think, "Did that come from that kid?"

Jason was in our high school's special-education program, having dealt all his life with autism—a brain disorder that limits one's range of activities and interests and impairs the ability to communicate, form relationships, and respond appropriately to the environment. Autism occurs mostly in boys and on a wide spectrum. Jason's one sibling, his older brother, Josh, is not autistic.

Jason did a pretty good job in his special-education classes and took pride in that. But according to Andy McCormack, his speech/language pathologist for four years at Greece Athena, Jason's challenges were considerable.

"He has a language-based learning disability that stems from his autism, and his verbal processing is extremely limited," Andy said. "His limited command of written and verbal skills carries into all other areas of learning. I would say his skills are that of a ten-year-old, or less, in most areas. When Jason came into our program, I was surprised at the classification of autism, because his outward signs are more that of classic mental retardation. But through the reports from his very early years, I could see the autism. The reports said he would flap his arms, kick his feet, not acknowledge other people in the room, become extremely overwhelmed by change, need repetition and structure, get upset when interrupted."

Characteristically, Jason talks louder than necessary and laughs longer than is appropriate. He also has a strong tendency toward what Andy terms "echolalia expression"—repeating what other people say.

"He would have trouble with social interaction, but his strength is that he can interact better than most people with autism," Andy said. "He loves the spotlight."

Jason's parents, David and Debbie, had struggled but never stopped advancing their mission of getting him accepted into mainstream activities—not an easy task, since young people can be harsh toward peers with disabilities and not every adult instructor or coach has the patience for accepting the challenges faced by an autistic person. I give J-Mac's parents a ton of credit for their insistence on seeking a social environment for their boy in which he didn't have to feel he was different.

He had come a long way socially by the time he reached his teens. Academically, Jason had not earned his high school equivalency by the time his class graduated, in June 2006, but he has continued taking classes through the Greece Central School District in hopes of one day reaching that goal.

One of the few classes in which Jason was mainstreamed was physical education. He was a pretty good runner and competed each fall on Athena's cross-country team. Jason was not among the top runners in the county, but was at least average and maybe even a little bit above average. He also ran outdoor track as a distance runner his first three years of high school.

Jason ran indoor track the winter of his freshman year. He discontinued that sport to become a regular part of our basketball program as a sophomore, thanks to a role that had been created for him by Jeff Amoroso, my junior varsity coach for nine years. Jeff did an outstanding job for me, winning close to eighty percent of his games. He was the one who really took Jason under his wing, and he deserves a lot of credit for that. The 2004–05 season was Jeff's last at Athena before he took his first head coaching job at Victor High School. He remains a physical education teacher at Athena as well as a good friend of mine.

Jason had been on Jeff's summer league team just prior to his sophomore year. He faithfully attended every game, getting a fair amount of playing time and occasionally scoring against competition that wasn't as strong as high school teams. When the school year started, Jason asked Jeff just about every day when basketball tryouts were.

It was clear to Jeff that Jason wasn't going to make the team, but he was determined to keep J-Mac around in some capacity, due to a very poignant phone message he got that fall from Debbie McElwain. Jason's mother pleaded with him to find some sort of spot for her son. It was such a heartfelt message, and I know Jeff kept it for a long time before erasing it.

"It's the kind of thing that for anybody who heard it, you kind of got choked up listening," Jeff said. "It was this plea wondering if there was any chance in my heart for him to be part of the team, because basketball is the only thing he thinks he's good at and it's kind of his identity."

I said to Jeff that if he wanted to keep Jason around in some capacity, it was up to him. I wasn't sure how I felt about the situation. On the one hand, as an educator you're obviously in the business to help kids; on the other, not everyone is reliable. For instance, a guidance counselor once came to me asking if I could involve an at-risk kid who liked basketball. I was willing to give him a chance, but he never showed up.

Would Jason be a distraction? During practices and games you need a minimum of distractions, regardless of their source. A manager is a regular part of the team and needs to augment what you want to do, not detract from it. But Jeff felt strongly enough about Jason's enthusiasm and desire that he offered him the team manager's position while cutting him as a player.

"I told him, 'I have a proposal. I'd like you to be our manager, in a different way—participate in practice every day, do our drills, be part of the team—but you just won't play in games,'" Jeff recalled. "Initially when I told him he'd been cut he was emotional, upset. But the proposal quickly changed his emotions into excitement."

I didn't spend a whole lot of time with Jason that year—my varsity team and his JVs would practice in the same gym on some occasions, or I'd see him when our teams traveled together. What

I observed was heartwarming, with Jason establishing himself as a full-fledged member of the team. The thing that I grew to appreciate about Jason is how loyal he was in everything I witnessed. As the season progressed, the JV kids became attached to him and really started establishing a bond with him. There's a tendency for some people to ridicule folks with disabilities, and earlier in his life Jason was definitely the target of some cruel treatment. But Jeff said the JV players treated him like a little brother and would not allow any cruelty. He got a prank or two played on him, but it was all in good fun.

I own the unofficial copyright as originator of Jason's nickname—not because I'm a renowned wordsmith, but because, frankly, I massacred his last name on a regular basis. It was a tongue twister to me; I just couldn't say it—"Mal-cal-wayne," "Mac-el-e-wane." Jeff would say, "Why can't you get it out—it's McElwain!" I said I had no idea. (The actual pronunciation is Mc-EL-wain. Many people still mispronounce it MAC-el-wain, with the emphasis on the first syllable instead of the second.)

My inspiration for Jason's nickname was Gerry McNamara, the great Syracuse University point guard. As a freshman, McNamara led the Orange to the 2003 NCAA championship by scoring six three-pointers in the first half of their 81-78 title-game win over Kansas. I said, "Jason, Syracuse has Gerry McNamara and everyone calls him G-Mac. So Greece Athena is going to have J-Mac."

It wouldn't have been as much fun if I was the only one who called him J-Mac, but everybody picked up on it and he liked it. Unless there are negative connotations, kids like nicknames, and nobody in this part of New York state would be ashamed to be linked to G-Mac. For years, Jason loved Kobe Bryant and signed his name "Jason 'Kobe' McElwain." But from that point on, the name J-Mac stuck like glue.

Jason came out for basketball again as a junior in 2004–05, this time for varsity. When it was time to make cuts, I did with him what I do whenever I cut a player: I brought him into the office for a few minutes and explained my decision. "Jason, you're not quite good enough to make the team," I said. "But I like your tremendous commitment to the program and would like to offer you the varsity manager's position." He definitely wanted to make the team, but at the same time he accepted being the manager very quickly—again.

Early that season I threw some trial and error at Jason to see how I could best use him as a manager. At first I had him do the plus-and-minus chart for our five-on-five drills. His duty was to track which players earned pluses for getting on the floor for a loose ball, getting an offensive rebound, taking the charge, or getting back on defense. The minuses would be for selfish play, taking a bad shot, not hustling back, and not blocking out.

After Jason did this once or twice, I realized it was too challenging for him and it wasn't going to work. Then I tried to get him to do some videography, but he struggled with that too— he would watch too much of the scrimmage and forget he was taping. So I had him run the clock. Even then, at a lot of practices I'd say, "J-Mac, two minutes on the clock," and find him on the side shooting baskets.

"J-Mac, come on back and do your job!"

"OK, Coach."

But by and large, he handled his tasks well and was happy to help in any way he could—running the clock, assisting in drills. He would help out in some drills as a passer and occasionally would get to do shooting drills, but he never really scrimmaged with us. I didn't have many one-on-one conversations with him. Still, I wanted to make sure he knew he was important to the team. He had some quirks, but to me he was just like any other kid. I never felt like he had a disability. Basically, I treated him no differently than any other player in the program, and I think he appreciated that.

This whole thing is about mentoring. People took me under their wing, and what it really gets down to is they turned my life around. They were people who saw my abilities and they mentored me. I find in case after case after case there is a person who sees an autistic person's talent and passion, and that's what attracts them. That's what this coach did. When you look at people on the autism spectrum, there is a mentor involved.

—Temple Grandin, best-selling author on living with autism

Jason was always very excited. He definitely had some difficulties and I could see he'd struggle at times with comprehension of what was socially acceptable; for instance, he'd get very emotional on the bench if we weren't doing well. But I never felt like he was going out of his way to be obnoxious. He was just a kid who wanted to be a part of the team any way he could.

I knew he had autism, but I did not know much about the disorder. As with many people, perhaps my best understanding of autism was through the movie *Rain Man*. The Dustin Hoffman character, Raymond Babbitt, would repeat things, especially those that gave him comfort, such as "Who's on first, What's on second" or asking for pancakes with maple syrup. Jason, meanwhile, always used to come up to Jeff Amoroso and ask him what time practice was and when tryouts began. As Jeff said, Jason would perseverate on pleasant thoughts, and once he locked in on something that was of particular interest, you could count on hearing about it a lot.

Jason doesn't have quite the need for structure that Rain Man has; he's certainly not going to demand that his underwear come from the Kmart in Cincinnati. He is able to carry on a fairly normal conversation, and he doesn't have the emotional distance of a Rain Man. But if the event or conversation taking place isn't interesting to him, he'll move right on to the next thing. That's just part of his autistic tendencies.

I'd take him on scouting trips sometimes, although it was hard for him to remain focused on the game because Athena wasn't playing. He likes being around basketball, and he would mingle. He was always getting scoops on different teams. Although autistic people have a tendency to be socially reclusive, that's not Jason's personality. He's not afraid to go up to people and meet them, and he's pretty bold when he wants an autograph.

I enjoyed his company on these scouting sessions. It was our way to build a better bond—he wasn't a playing member of the team, but we wanted him to feel included and this was a way I could show my appreciation. Besides, I always had fun talking to him. He was not only into our team, but he was into basketball in general. He loves to talk, and it's a blast listening to what he has to say—if you've got the time.

I think the relationship that a coach has with a player or a manager, each of those relationships is a real bond, an emotional relationship.

—Jim Larranaga, head basketball coach, George Mason University

---

Jason and I were extremely similar in that basketball was the basis for our respective missions in life. Jeff Amoroso refers to Jason, very appropriately, as a basketball nomad. He knew about players from all over town—who was good, all the starters of the teams we were playing. He had all these contacts and associations with kids on other teams and they would give him information, anything that he thought might help our team. He'd get on the Internet constantly; he was really into e-mailing and text messaging. He was so in tune with the local basketball scene, he could tell you the starting lineups of every team we played in Monroe County.

In fact, at times Jason would be a step ahead of me. Once during his senior year I was going over game preparation, and my scouting report on our opponent was a month old. As I mentioned one player, Jason piped up, "Coach, he's not on the team anymore. He quit last week." I think he really took great pride in knowing what was going on with all the teams.

He's a kid who's huge into sports, watching ESPN's *SportsCenter* practically every day. He certainly isn't ignorant of what's going on in baseball or football, and students have told me that they played Little League baseball with Jason. But basketball is what he lives and breathes. He can still tell you the starting lineups of the top twenty Division I basketball colleges. I thought I was a hoops aficionado, but I could not name the starters for George Mason in 2006. One of our huge debates on the 2005–06 Greece Athena team was over who was the better player—J. J. Redick, of Duke, or Adam Morrison, of Gonzaga. Jason was always right in the middle of those discussions.

J-Mac hung out quite a bit with the rest of the kids on the team. Many times they'd go to his house for video games and snacks. Jason was the "snacks king"—he'd bring all kinds of snacks to games and practices, and it was almost an expectation that he would have Gatorade or some kind of chips or snack bars for everyone. He had quite a stash at home that his family would buy for him. The first time I was in his house, I noticed it was stocked with all kinds of food. I'm not sure his mom and dad knew he was always passing those snacks along to the rest of the team.

He tends to mimic people because of his autism, and a lot of the things he's repeated have originated out of my mouth. So, I felt it was very important that he mimic me in a positive way. As a leader, you must be aware that your people are going to adopt what you're all about—what you believe, your level of integrity. They're looking to you and that's a powerful level of responsibility.

Jim would understand the value of having a guy like Jason on the team, the value it had for the other players. I could see how Jim would use this for a life lesson. I've known from the first day of coaching with Jim in Rochester, he's one of those guys I labeled as "He just gets it." We all have an opportunity to affect a lot of lives, and that's what he does.

—Jay Wright, head basketball coach, Villanova University

Jason came to take part enthusiastically in practices and yell encouragement and instruction from the bench during games, just like I did. Typically, by the final buzzer the tail of his dress shirt would be hanging all the way out. He was so into the game that he would become massively disheveled, and it was hilarious watching his teammates help put him back together.

I love how my emphasis on teamwork and family filtered down to J-Mac and his teammates, as exhibited by the way they treated him with such respect. One of our tri-captains, Steve Kerr, basically took Jason under his wing and eventually began volunteering with the special-education program at Athena. That kind of thing just gratifies a coach to no end, in terms of what he or she is trying to convey to the kids about caring for each other.

J-Mac knew these guys really well. The senior captains—Kerr, Levar Goff, and Rickey Wallace—were not only talented but also had nice relationships with Jason. Everybody did, really.

"I felt like J-Mac wasn't a manager to me. I never really pictured him as that," Terrance McCutchen said. "He was the sixteenth man on the team; he was a part of it."

"He put in a lot of work, getting up at six a.m. for practice just to play his role as manager," Rickey Wallace said. "He just had so much passion—to see us do well, to help out."

Over his three years with the Athena basketball program it was great to see J-Mac develop as a human being, just as his mom had hoped for during that phone message for Jeff Amoroso. In my eyes, he evolved and matured right along with the rest of the team, establishing some nice camaraderie.

It wasn't just that he was a part of the basketball team. He was also developing relationships that he'll have the rest of his life. Here was a social situation that was like a refuge for him—being with a group of guys on a daily basis for more than four months straight. Most high-schoolers are trying to find a niche, and it's easy to feel isolated and like an outcast, especially when you have special needs.

By encouraging Jason to fulfill his mission of being the best team manager around, I was making an extension of my own mission. I've come to appreciate how this experience was a living example of all the life-lesson quotes I like to use.

Last but certainly not least, Jason's presence rubbed off on the players. These kids became almost like his big brothers. They looked out for him and took care of him—made sure his tie was tied, made sure his shirt was tucked in. They developed a new sense of mission about tolerance, caring for your fellow man, and loving your neighbor. The bottom line is, having Jason in our midst was a win-win situation for everybody.

ACTION STEP: *Write down your values and what is most important to you. Do a little self-reflection; spend some time alone. From there, develop a mission statement. For instance, my mission statement is about being an outstanding role model, being a positive influence in the world by helping make others' dreams come true. Having that in words really helps me make my choices in life and discern whether a choice would help or hinder my mission. Keep in mind that it's a good idea to go back periodically and reevaluate that statement for possible updates and revisions, since your mission evolves as life circumstances change.*

three

Set Goals

How do you achieve your mission? How do you set about getting there? How will you apply the self-discipline necessary to reach your goals?

BACK WHEN HE WAS A SOPHOMORE, J-MAC BECAME such a valued part of the junior varsity that Jeff Amoroso eventually sought to put him in an actual game. Jeff found he could do so without skirting the rules of our local high school athletic governing body, Section 5, because Jason had participated in the required number of practices even though he wasn't a roster player. So, after getting approval from our athletic director, Randy Hutto, Jeff activated Jason for the squad's final home game, against Irondequoit.

J-Mac's big moment arrived when he entered play with about 2:15 left and his team up by fourteen points. He missed his only shooting attempt, a three-pointer. But he was fouled on the play, even though he only got run into slightly. It was clear that the refs were taking liberties with what constitutes an actual foul in an effort to help Jason get into the scoring column.

He made all of his free throws and the place erupted. It shouldn't come as a major surprise that he converted from the foul line—shooting is easily the best aspect of his game—but he'd never experienced the pressure of a crowd looking on. So everybody was excited in the locker room that he had come through, and the buzz got around school a little bit in the aftermath. I think everybody got a big kick out of it.

"He buried all three of them," Jeff Amoroso recalled. "It was a proud, crowning moment. I remember not being able to address my team at the end of the game, I got so choked up. You always hope something like that works out for the best, and it did. Then, for the team banquet, I got a plaque for him saying, 'Career free-throw shooting leader in Athena High School history.' Jason's eyes welled up with tears and he got a nice ovation."

That plaque does tell the truth. By going three for three from the line, he shot one hundred percent, and you can't beat that, so he will eternally be at least tied for the all-time school lead.

Jason's feat evoked strong memories of the 1993 movie *Rudy* and the real-life title character's dream of getting into just one University of Notre Dame football game—not the whole game; just a play or two. Jason making his three points was like Rudy making his tackle at the movie's end. Those seemingly commonplace occurrences were enough to make onlookers go bananas, because everyone knew how hard those underdogs had worked for their chance to shine.

J-Mac's few moments in the spotlight whetted his appetite for pursuing a more permanent playing arrangement at Athena. All the other team managers I've had would just show up for practice and games, which was all I really expected of them. But Jason was unique in that he not only wanted to rise above his manager's role and make the team; he was willing to commit to a lot of off-season stuff too. That's what he did between his sophomore and junior seasons as well as his junior and senior years, participating in town camps and playing pickup games every free moment he had. After school started up again, he'd compete in fall basketball leagues and work them around his cross-country schedule.

Yet by the time tryouts rolled around, even though I felt that Jason had improved, his playing ability was still noticeably below that of the other kids on our team. For starters, when he came out for his junior season he was five feet six and 120 pounds. He had grown maybe an inch by the time he was a senior. It didn't help his chances that we had very good, talented clubs in both 2004–05 and 2005–06.

Going into his senior season, Jason went through the summer committed to trying to make the team once more despite those overwhelming odds. He even went with us to a summer camp at St. Bonaventure University, the first time he had ever attended an overnight camp with the team.

At no time did I think there was a great chance he would make the cut as a senior, but I didn't want to tell him not to try out. Basketball was such a great avenue for Jason and he so dearly wanted to be a part of the team, and we all liked having him. Most other kids with limited talent—and those who possess abundant talent, for that matter—don't have the burning desire to be connected with their team like Jason did. How do you tell somebody with that kind of devotion that it's not in his best interests to try out?

So once again he tried out for the varsity, in the fall of 2005. I really admired that he tried out for basketball three straight years without making it. In fact, you don't usually see kids try out more than once. A second time is rare, and I don't ever recall a kid who tried out a third time after having been cut twice. You've really got to admire Jason's determination and perseverance. And even though he was smaller than just about everybody else and I'm sure he got his share of bumps and bruises, he was a gritty kid and never took himself out of a scrimmage with an injury.

In terms of playing ability, he had a pretty good shot and could score when the competition wasn't so tough, when he didn't have to dribble very much and wasn't guarded by someone who was a much better athlete than he. He would pass when necessary and I never got the impression that he was selfish—but he definitely had a mind-set that if he had an opening, he was going to fire the rock. He liked to shoot and liked to score. I remember that in his fall league he would get a great thrill whenever he scored. His shot was very high arching—not a jump shot but more of a push shot, which made it more susceptible to getting blocked. But he somewhat offset that problem by having a fairly quick release.

He had good endurance from his cross-country background but was not particularly quick; he didn't have that real burst of speed. Though he could shoot decently, he lacked ball-handling skills. He couldn't do anything off the dribble, especially if someone was on him tight. He would have trouble anytime people put pressure on him. He certainly played with enthusiasm, but his small stature was a natural detriment on both offense and defense, and it didn't help that he couldn't jump well. Because of his learning disability, he also had difficulty comprehending some of our strategies, like a motion offense.

Add up all his shortcomings, and I had to cut him again as a senior. I'm sure that for a few seconds he got that awful sinking feeling in the pit of his stomach, hearing that once more all his sweat and toil during the previous several months was not enough to make a difference.

But this time, I had a pleasant surprise in store to offset his disappointment at the bad news. I was very quick to tell him, "Jason, I'd like to keep you in the same role as team manager and also give you a gift this year. I'm going to get you a uniform and, hopefully, get you into a game." I didn't exactly guarantee him playing time, but hoped that I could at least put him on the active roster for Senior Night.

Actually, I think Jason came into my office almost expecting that he'd be cut, because by that point most players pretty much know where they stand. Even so, nobody wants to hear those words, and in Jason's case, he was hearing them for the third straight November. I'm sure he felt he'd been dealt a bad hand, having incessantly pursued his monumental goal only to come up short every year.

However, he had never anticipated that I'd offer to try and suit him up. That brightened his spirits pretty quickly, and he again bounced back from his disappointment with a renewed enthusiasm as team manager. He now had a new goal, which was to see a few minutes of live varsity competition.

Similarities between Jason and Rudy are uncanny. Every year Rudy accepted his role of practicing with the team in hopes that one day he'd suit up and play. He was the smallest player on the squad but the one who never gave up, who wasn't going to be denied. Rudy had that unshakable focus on his dream. In the same way, Jason would ask me almost every day if his uniform had come in. Truth be told, I didn't yet know where we were even going to find one, since I only had enough available for the guys I kept on the roster. We'd probably have to scrounge around a bit for an old uniform.

Yet there was one goal for Jason that loomed even larger than any individual pursuit, and it was the same goal that remained front and center for me: winning sectionals. Jason was our biggest cheerleader as we worked toward ascending that mountain. "We've got to stay focused" became his mantra in his senior year, 2005–06. It gratifies me that he has always put the team at the top of his priority list.

J-Mac's involvement as a team manager grew even more that season. He became accustomed to giving input like you'd normally see from a head coach, captain, or assistant coach. For instance, I would end practice and usually finish with some comments—

how things went, where we needed to improve from there, and a reminder to get a good night's rest the day before a game. Then I would ask if anybody else had comments, and Jason would almost always have something to say—usually repeating what I had just said. The kids would say things like, "J-Mac, we just covered that"; "J-Mac, that's enough." Earlier in Jason's career, it was comical. By his senior year it got to the point that the kids knew what to expect, and they simply rolled with it. That's just one example of how Jason's tendencies may be off-putting to those who don't know him well, but over time, they begin to realize that's just an example of his autistic traits and there's really nothing wrong with it.

"His 'Thirty-two minutes; give it your all'—the kids would giggle a little bit, but at the same time they wanted him to say it. It was almost funny to see how passionate he was," said Mike Setzer, my JV coach, who is very close with J-Mac. "But he was serious about what he said. On game day he was always the most nervous one. So if somebody was joking around he would say, 'Are you ready today, are you ready today?' He just lives and drinks basketball, and he's an adorable kid. He's one of the most likable kids you're ever going to meet; you can't help but like him. Jason would visit me every other day during study time and we would talk about the Athena game coming up. I'd ask who he thought the key matchups were going to be and just let him talk. It was just always fun to talk basketball with him. Whenever he would leave the room, I'd say, 'Jay, who loves ya?' He'd say, 'Coach Setzer.'"

Mike also had the responsibility of keeping somewhat of an eye on Jason during games. "It wasn't like it was a job of mine. I did that because I wanted to," he said. "But we always had to keep track of Jason. He would get very emotional on the sideline; Jason is all about emotion. If the other team was on a run, he couldn't handle it. Jason wanted to say something and I would just pat him on the back—'It's all right, it's all right.' He'd go, 'Why are we losing? Why are we losing?' And if we lost, Jason wore those losses on his sleeve harder than everybody. Jason's dad and I would talk and he'd say, 'Thank God you're there, because he would get a technical foul.'

"The only time he would ever show sign of real anger," Mike added, "was when the other fans would taunt Athena—like if the other team was beating us and their fans starting chanting 'O-ver-rat-ed, o-ver-rat-ed.' Well, now Jason's going to want to go after them. He was that much of a team guy. If somebody said something bad about our team or one of the players, he wouldn't allow for that. You wouldn't dare say something bad about Athena!"

I respected J-Mac immensely. Basketball is the ultimate team sport, and he came every day to try to help our team get better and be successful. He was willing to pretty much do anything he could. He only missed one game in three years and it was due to illness. I remember Rickey Wallace saying after a practice Jason missed around that time, "You know, Coach, it's not the same without J-Mac."

Jason was as consistent as any team member, if not more so. He showed up like clockwork every day for practice and for every game. Plus, he was always looking ahead to bigger and brighter things—for Athena, not for himself as an individual. It was all about the team. My guess is that he thought about Greece Athena basketball as he drifted off to sleep at night and when he woke up in the morning. Chances are, he'd imagine what it would be like for our team to hoist a championship trophy with him being right in the thick of it all.

"We've got to stay focused, we've got to stay focused." Toward season's end in 2005–06 we fed off the power of Jason's focus, feeling we were going to achieve that goal of winning a sectional championship and there was no stopping us.

＊

J-Mac wasn't alone in setting a sectional title as his supreme goal. I had never enjoyed one as a player, and as a coach I'd been waiting for one longer than J-Mac had been alive.

I entered the 2005–06 season with a career record of 233-169 over 19 years, with the bulk of my success having come more recently. My teams had won or tied for Monroe County league titles in 1996, 2002, 2003, and 2005. Three times I've taken over losing programs and they've become winners in short periods of time—at Le Roy, Greece Olympia, and Greece Athena. I've had winning seasons in all but one year since 1992–93.

Hopefully I've made clear already that my mission is not about winning and winning alone. Through both up and down times, it's hugely important to keep in mind that there's so much more to coaching. You're trying to get a group of people to work together—consider how in the workplace job status often hinges just as much on the ability to get along with others as the ability to perform tasks. At the beginning of each season I have a team meeting at my house and we set goals for the season. When I work on individual goals with the players, the general objective is for them to improve not only as athletes but also as members of society.

On the other hand, let's face it—in terms of how a coach is measured, success on the court is often an apt indicator that you're carrying out your mission well. My first year as a varsity coach, we won one whole game; I didn't return the next year. Another year early on in my career, we won two games. Sometimes the talent level isn't there; sometimes it's a chemistry issue. One way or another, it's a very long season when you're not racking up the W's. There's always that bottom line. Coaching can be capricious in the sense that people are very fickle with you. When things are going well, you're the best thing since sliced bread—and when they're not going well, people are trying to figure out how they can move you out of there. I suppose high school coaches enjoy more job insulation than at the Division I or professional level, but expectations from parents and fans can still be mighty intense.

Except for my early years I've been extremely satisfied with my regular-season accomplishments. Few varsity coaches can say that they've significantly upgraded three programs in their careers. I feel like I've gained plenty of respect around the Monroe County league and Section 5 for my coaching abilities, and I'd like to think that young men entering Greece Athena High School realize they're joining a quality basketball program.

But in a way, all the regular-season success made my lack of a sectional championship even more of an Achilles' heel—a glaring omission that every coach seeks to overcome so as to achieve validation, a burden that grows heavier each year. You often hear about the best golfer, football coach, baseball player, and so on who "never won the big one." In terms of my personal goals, that one stuck out like a sore thumb.

Even worse, a sectional title had narrowly eluded me on more occasions than I care to remember. My teams had been to the Section 5 semifinals six times without ever reaching a final, losing four of those games in the last thirty seconds. The first time you reach a Final Four, you're happy that you've advanced a notch. You figure reaching a final and winning a championship are the next natural steps, perhaps in the next year or two. But for me, even though I had some excellent teams, year after year they hit the same wall in the semifinal round. For every season that my squads were sent home earlier than expected, I got that same sick feeling that I'm sure Jason experienced every time he was told he'd been cut from the team. And then I had eight months until the next season to dwell on my failures.

Perhaps my lowest point occurred in 2003–04, when we coughed up an eight-point lead with three minutes to go against

Greece Arcadia in the sectional semifinals. It had seemed such a sure thing that Jeff Amoroso, my assistant at the time, actually turned to me and said it looked like we were finally going to clear that hurdle.

I remember going home to my wife after that loss and absolutely losing it: "Why can't I get through this barrier? What am I doing as a coach that at the end of the game, we aren't making the big shot or the big rebound?" I went on for a good hour, very upset and distraught. Some extended profanity came out of my mouth, which is very rare for me, and Pat was shocked to see me lose control of myself for that long a stretch.

To me, life was unfair, and I really questioned why God was doing this to me. Did I place too much emphasis on integrity and treating people fairly? Might I get better results if I were a slave driver who cussed out the players and refs day in and day out, caring about winning and nothing but? At that point it seemed like the better option.

But by 2005–06, there was strong cause for hope again. I had a team of high character, from the stars on down to the team manager. It was a talented club as well, possibly the best I'd ever had—one that could very well end my career-long sectional title drought. Steve Kerr, Rickey Wallace, and Levar Goff had all been starters for my 2004–05 varsity, which finished 15-5 overall and won the Monroe County Division II title. As my tri-captains, they would go on to combine for more than two-thirds of our points in 2005–06. We also had some great talent from the 2004–05 junior varsity, which finished 17-1 under Mike Setzer. In a word, we were loaded.

It was my twenty-fifth straight year of coaching. I couldn't be happier doing what I loved in the town of Greece, where I grew up, surrounded by close family, longtime friends, and a great team. There was seemingly no better time to be a coach. Who wouldn't be excited about the possibilities that lay ahead?

Well, I wasn't, for one. Incredibly, I was suddenly looking to depart the coaching ranks almost before the season had begun.

ACTION STEP: *List on paper as many goals as you can in thirty minutes. You may not reach all of them, nor should you expect to. But have at least one breakthrough goal, something that's really going to make you stretch. Think of the person you'd need to become in order to reach that goal. Your goals could be related to anything—health, occupation, family, spiritual life, finances, athletics, academics. They may change over time; goals from three years ago might be unimportant now. But that's the evolution of life. The main thing, as motivational expert Zig Ziglar says, is that "you can't hit a target you cannot see, and you cannot see a target you do not have."*

four

Persevere

How do you keep from getting knocked off your goals? If you do encounter roadblocks, are you willing to take action and explore alternate routes?

I HADN'T BEEN ABLE TO SLEEP FOR THREE STRAIGHT nights. I was struggling.

That's not like me at all. Sometimes after a very difficult loss I might toss and turn a little bit, but I've always been able to sleep.

All day long I was tired, irritable, confused, shaken up. I didn't feel good at school. Once, I even had a car accident on my way home from practice. I came too fast around a bend, lost control, and caused a fender bender. Though icy road conditions were certainly a factor, the mishap likely could have been avoided if I hadn't been distracted by the controversy swirling around me.

That's how the worst conflict I've ever had in coaching was affecting me, and it had me on the verge of filing my resignation. My life had not been the same since December 5, 2005, when I emerged from a late-afternoon scrimmage at Greece Athena and found myself in the foyer face-to-face with at least ten parents. Nobody was smiling.

"We need to talk to you," they said. It was completely unscheduled and my first thought was, "Oh my God, what's going on?"

Our season had been going fine up to that point, or so I'd thought. We'd won our first two games, and except for needing to make an adjustment or two on defense, I felt very good about where we were going, and everyone else was excited. We were getting ready to face two strong league opponents, Irondequoit and Webster Thomas, at home in our first regular-season games and I liked our chances. Really, I thought this was a team that had the potential to win the league and sectional titles. Certainly it wasn't the first time I'd felt that way, but I was very optimistic.

That all changed in the blink of an eye when I encountered the posse of parents. What had apparently fueled their action was a tiny article the previous morning in our local daily newspaper, the *Democrat and Chronicle*. It described how we had won our season-opening tournament that weekend, but in naming the key contributors it neglected to note that John Swartz, one of my seniors, had made the all-tournament team.

The scores had been called in by Kelvin Goff, my assistant coach. Usually I would call the scores in, but sometimes he would if I needed to meet with a player or something similar.

We got a nice headline: WALLACE, GOFF PROPEL ATHENA TO CHAMPIONSHIP. The article, with the box score underneath, read:

Rickey Wallace and Levar Goff combined for 48 points as Greece Athena defeated Gates Chili 66-48 in the championship game of the Greece Olympia Tournament on Saturday. Goff had 23 points, four steals and two assists. Wallace, the tournament MVP, had 25 points and two steals for the Trojans (2-0). With Athena trailing by 10 in the second quarter, Kourtney Goff, brother of Levar, came off the bench and scored four points as the Trojans cut the lead to five at halftime. Athena closed the third quarter with an 8-0 run to lead 45-39.

That was all factually correct, and to the casual observer there was no apparent problem with the story. But John Swartz had made the all-tournament team and Kourtney hadn't. Swartz rarely ever got mentioned, and since he was not one of our stars, I remember cringing and thinking, "Wow, it would've been nice if he had been in the article." When I report scores to the newspaper I try to get kids named who maybe haven't gotten much ink. The more you can do that, the more it's going to help team chemistry.

But on that night, my assistant coach—who also happened to be Levar and Kourtney's dad—had called the scores in. The morning after the story appeared, John Swartz's dad, John, was waiting for me when I showed up at my office at Greece Athena. He was visibly upset.

"Kelvin must have called the game in to the paper, because my son was slighted," he said.

I talked to him for five or six minutes and got him calmed down. I told him, "I did not hear what Kelvin said to the paper, but you talk about numerous things when you call something in, and what they end up printing is their discretion. But to make you feel better, I would be glad to call in the games from now on instead of Kelvin."

As my volunteer assistant who was beginning his sixth season, Kelvin had been loyal and hardworking. He had a job in a machine shop and worked different shifts, but would come to practices as much as possible and worked his schedule out so that he never missed games. I remember that during our February break, he would come to morning practice straight from the night shift and then go home to bed.

But due to his strong personality, Kelvin wasn't always a hit. It was not unusual for him to get into small confrontations with parents or referees, though he was levelheaded toward the players and me.

Now the parents' discomfort had hit a new high because Kelvin's sons, Levar, a senior guard, and Kourtney, a sophomore guard, were both on the varsity and Kelvin was unabashedly their biggest fan. And in that small newspaper write-up, Levar and Kourtney were both mentioned, even though Kourtney hadn't made all-tournament.

Looking back, I guess I should have known something was brewing, because Mr. Swartz's complaint was the second warning sign I'd gotten during our young season. The week before our first game, Barb Kerr, the mother of one of my tri-captains and with whom I have a pretty good relationship, had asked to talk to me.

"What's up?" I responded.

"We really have a concern with Kelvin sitting on the bench during games."

"Well, he's been doing it for five or six years. I appreciate your giving me the information, but Kelvin's been a loyal supporter for a long time," I replied. She didn't debate it with me, and it wasn't a long conversation. So I shrugged it off.

As it turned out, that exchange plus the one with Mr. Swartz set the stage for my personal Black Monday. Here I was in the high school hallway on December 5, facing parents of eleven of my fifteen players. Never had a group approached me like that in more than twenty years of coaching high school basketball.

I took them into a classroom and we sat down for almost thirty minutes. They made it very clear that they felt Kelvin's role as assistant coach presented a conflict of interest. It was obvious that their feelings were also fueled by Kelvin's tendency to rub people the wrong way.

But they were being pretty nervy suggesting I remove him as coach, since I was the one running the team. As the meeting unfolded, I was able to connect the dots to their main grievance: They felt Kelvin's presence on the bench during games was affecting my choices regarding who saw playing time. More specifically, they felt I was favoring Kelvin's sons. They didn't come right out and say it, but they didn't have to.

I was amazed at how this simple little newspaper story could cause such a ruckus. I truly don't believe Kelvin was out to promote his sons at the other players' expense. For all I knew, he had mentioned John Swartz and other players to the newspaper and there simply wasn't enough space to include all those details in the write-up.

In that parents' meeting I basically just tried to listen to what they had to say. I didn't immediately indicate to them that I would remove Kelvin. I needed time to figure that part out. I said that I understood their concerns and would meet with my staff about it. I walked away thinking, "Wow, this is a much bigger issue than I thought." I was shocked that this many parents were upset. What threw me is that there had been pretty solid camaraderie among the parents and coaches at our preseason meeting.

What also threw me was that it wasn't as if they were saying, "Hey, you're playing the wrong players and now we're 0-2." We had *won* our season-opening tournament—we were 2-0! I remember that earlier in my career, as long as I stayed around .500 the expectations weren't too high and people basically left me alone. I'm proud of my more recent success, but in some respects maybe I created a monster. How else could you explain having a heap of trouble after a 2-0 start and several winning seasons in a row?

Actually, the rumblings had begun before Kourtney's arrival on varsity. There was never any real issue with how Kelvin treated the other players, but the potential nepotism factor created a steadily growing chasm between him and the other parents. Even so, his son Levar was such an engaging kid and good player that parents had been able to overlook their friction with his dad. But now Kourtney was with us, and the parents seemed to feel that as a sophomore he hadn't paid sufficient dues for the honor of being mentioned in print. For them, that little article was the last straw.

The day after the parent meeting, on December 6, Kelvin showed up toward the end of our practice and I met with him, relaying the parents' feelings. He was shocked, disappointed, furious—very upset. I said I completely understood.

I felt I had three choices, and none were completely effective: Go with the status quo and don't do anything about Kelvin, thereby losing the parents; remove him as an assistant coach, thereby losing my own authority to run the team; or offer to keep Kelvin on as coach in practices but not in a coaching capacity during games, thereby running the risk of losing him. No matter what, I was going to lose something.

In fact, something had already been lost: the parents' belief in my personal integrity, and possibly my players' belief as well. That was absolutely devastating to me. It was the worst thing ever to happen to me in coaching or any other part of my life in basketball. Now all my personal ideals were being questioned, despite the weekly life lessons I had put out there.

Objectively speaking, I did have to ask myself if the parents indeed had a point—was it at all possible that Kelvin was influencing me? But I never felt he had inappropriately guided my decision making at any time.

My immediate thought was to perhaps step down. I've never been a quitter, but more so than ever before, I really had to weigh just how important coaching was in my life.

I talked to my wife and fellow coaches about whether I should resign. I wasn't just bothered by the integrity issue. Kelvin had been a good coach and friend and I wanted to support him, and I felt he was being treated way too harshly by the other parents. For a high school coach to resign during the season is very rare, but I wasn't fearful about whether my decision was going to get bad publicity. It simply came down to what the right thing was for me to do.

Leaving certainly would have put my JV coach, Mike Setzer, in a difficult position, since chances are he would have filled in for me. That's quite a mess he would have been inheriting for his first varsity job. Besides, he had no interest in succeeding me in such a manner. He told me, "Jim, this program needs you."

Mike was so helpful in that he was a very good listener; I leaned on him during this difficult stretch. I also got a lot of support from Mike's predecessor, Jeff Amoroso, who still teaches at Athena. At times I would also discuss the issue with my friends Mike Butler, Rob Cerone, and Stan Cipura, all of whom I share office space with at Athena. There were usually two, three, or four of us hashing out what was going on. Randy Hutto, my athletic director, was very supportive as well.

How would I fill my time if I resigned? Certainly I could spend more time with my family and my hobbies, areas that get compromised time-wise because of coaching. Plus, I'd still be working with high-schoolers as a physical education teacher, enjoying that teacher-student connection.

But was this the life I wanted? Coaching was so much in my blood. I got a chance to be associated with all different kinds of great people, and it would have been very strange not doing that anymore. And despite all our internal team problems, I didn't want to lose that bond with the kids. I really wanted to guide them.

I had one particularly good talk with my dad. Normally during the season things are very regimented, and because of the time factor I don't get to chat with my parents as much as I'd like. But I remember telling him at length what was happening and how very frustrated I was, that the parents were not letting me coach the team. My dad, who had been my own head coach at Greece Arcadia, said, "You've had difficult parents before. You have to stay strong and do what you think is right." And that was good, sound advice.

The strongest message that I should stay on as coach came from my wife. At the time, Pat and I had been married nearly twenty-four years, so she had seen all of the ups and downs of my career. She's missed very few of my games—meaning that at times, she and other family members have had to hear critiques and observations in the stands that are very difficult to hear about somebody you love.

Pat is not someone who's deeply immersed in the X's and O's of the game; I'm not going to come home and hear her ask, "How come you went to a zone defense?" But she's a physical education teacher at Brockport High School, so she can appreciate scholastic sports, and she also has a lot of wisdom. So what she told me during my crisis period really stuck.

If Pat had said, "Yeah, I think it's best for you to quit," then that's what I believe I would have done. But instead she said, "Jim, I think it's a decision you'll regret the rest of your life. Your mission is to be an outstanding role model, and the message you'd be sending is that you're a quitter." Pat emphasized that God had put me on this earth to make my athletes' lives better: "Don't ever let anyone take you away from your passion and your life."

That was a period when I really turned to my faith, probably becoming even more consistent in praying every single day, asking God just to help me get through this. After a few days I came to realize that now was the time to step up and walk the walk, because I had talked the talk with my players about persevering and never giving up. From that point on, I became determined to coach this basketball team to the best of my ability. There was no turning back.

On December 7, two days after the parent meeting, I held a players-only meeting right after school. I told them, "We have an issue we have to get out if we're going to keep this team together." I shared what had come out of the parents' meeting—and found out that most of the kids were uncomfortable with Kelvin Goff on the bench as well. Kourtney was very upset by this acknowledgment and Levar was more in shock. They had always admired their father, because he cared so deeply about them. The meeting was tough for Rickey Wallace too, because he was very tight with the Goffs.

During this tense discussion, J-Mac spoke up very strongly for Kelvin: "Mr. Goff is a good man, a good coach, and should stay in the role he's in now." I'll never forget that. Jason was tremendously supportive of having Mr. Goff stay, but most of the players felt differently.

We put it to an anonymous vote, with three options: Did they want to see Kelvin step down completely as coach? Did they want Kelvin to only coach in practice but not be on the bench during games? Or did they want to maintain the status quo, with no change at all? I counted the votes and announced the results right then and there: Two-thirds had asked for Kelvin to coach the team in practice but not in games. I told them I would go along with that, even though I suspected that some of the players were just parroting their parents' feelings.

Right after the meeting, I gave Kelvin the news. We had always gotten along well, but he was so upset that since that moment, my relationship with him has never been the same.

That night I contacted all the parents and said we needed to meet. I reached Kelvin and he was still pretty disgruntled, but he agreed to come. Finally, he was going to come face-to-face with the folks who had wanted his role reduced. I didn't sleep well at all that night—that may have been my worst night, wondering how this was all going to turn out.

The meeting took place before our Thursday evening practice on December 8. At least one parent of every player attended, including both Kelvin and his wife. It didn't take long for things to become very emotional and heated. There were even questions raised about whether this was a race issue, and it's true that our situation was very delicate because it pitted a black coach, Kelvin, against an almost completely Caucasian group of parents.

People see coaches on television and they see the TV lights, the NCAA tournament run. It's enjoyable and exciting, but there's a world out there they don't see.

—Jay Wright, head basketball coach, Villanova University

I made very clear that the decision about Kelvin not remaining on the bench during games was based on player input, not parental input. Thankfully, we had to begin our practice, so that's how I brought the meeting, which had lasted a bit over an hour, to a close. Kelvin did not join us at the beginning of practice, but otherwise it was business as usual—until he came in during the first drill, took his sons out of practice ("We're not playing for Athena," he said), and walked out with them. The team was somewhat shocked, saying things like, "I hope they're not going to leave for good."

The next morning, Kelvin called me and said that his sons would be at school and practice that day, but he was still very distraught. Levar and Kourtney did show up for practice—without their dad, who had decided that his days as a coach were over. At least we were fortunate to have his sons back: I found out that Kelvin had met with Randy Hutto, our athletic director, about transferring Levar and Kourtney to another school, but he learned they wouldn't be eligible to play that season. I really think he wanted his sons to continue playing at Athena, but he was just hurt and struggling with the whole situation.

Now I had another problem as well: how to hold team chemistry together. As is usually the case in these kinds of parent-coach struggles, the athletes found themselves caught in the middle.

"We didn't know what was going to happen—didn't know who was going to be on our team, who was going to be coach," recalled Terrance McCutchen, a junior guard that season.

Keeping everyone happy is especially tough in basketball, what with only five players on the court at one time—far fewer than in soccer or football. Most varsity basketball teams play seven to nine different kids when the game is on the line, and the other five or six won't ever go into a game in that kind of situation.

Along with wins and losses, the biggest heat a coach takes is over playing time. You certainly have to expect controversy and criticism if you're going to get into coaching, and I've had my share. Over the years the issues have ranged from racial prejudice to violation of team rules, from wondering why we're not winning more to players not getting the ball passed to them enough.

But the biggest concern for players, and definitely for parents, is playing time. Even if it's presented as some other concern, it almost always comes back to that. The Goff situation was a perfect example. Whereas Levar was an established starter, Kourtney was a sophomore substitute. That didn't sit well with the parents of my juniors and seniors, who felt that Kourtney should have stayed on the junior varsity and shouldn't be eating into their own kids' PT.

Adding to my dilemma in early 2005–06 was the fact that I had several very talented players who were used to playing all the time. They and their parents arrived at the varsity level with a false sense of security when, in fact, making that jump from JV and getting immediate playing time is often difficult. The kids are not ready to take a completely different role. It may be the first time they've ever had to sit on the bench. Johnny was a starter in seventh, eighth, and ninth grade, and now he's not only not starting—he's not even playing. He's being told, "Guess what? You've got to wait your turn."

That disappointment carries right over to the parents and may even be greater for them. It's a blow not only to Johnny's ego, but to the family's ego too. It gives Mom and Dad less standing among other parents and their coworkers. Every parent wants to be able to say that their son is starting or at least playing a fair amount. Whenever people live through their kids like that, their perspective on things can become quite warped. Even the most stellar of community members can become very irrational. In fact, early in my coaching career I caught grief from my own principal for not playing his son.

Hoosiers, which I've seen several times and which is considered one of the greatest sports movies ever made, is a film I can well relate to regarding what the Gene Hackman character, Coach Norman Dale, endured with parents and townspeople. Not unlike Coach Dale's, my instinct in December 2005 was to stick to my guns and do what I thought was best for the team. Also like Norman Dale, the price I paid was that I often felt like I stood alone.

Hoosiers is based on a true story about an Indiana high school team from the 1950s. It illustrates that tensions between coaches and parents in scholastic sports have a long history, but I'd also venture that this trend has ballooned in recent years. Parental control issues in education are now such that lawsuits are right around the corner if a teacher or coach touches or verbally abuses a student. Thus, educators have become more apprehensive about asserting themselves.

That's made it more and more difficult to run a quality basketball program. Dealing with difficult parents is now becoming the harshest reality and greatest challenge of coaching, and it's happening throughout scholastic athletics—especially in sports that are more in the limelight, like basketball. It really drains you. It wears down coaches, and a lot of my cohorts have gotten out for that reason.

I need to make clear that this syndrome does not apply to the majority of players' parents I've known over the years. To suggest otherwise would give the impression that I'm thin skinned and paranoid. As a coach it's essential that I build good relationships with my players, and the process is made so much easier when their parents are on the same page. I've really enjoyed the camaraderie with hundreds of parents who have supported my basketball programs through thick and thin. They volunteer for various team activities and are truly interested in our success, though of course they'd like to see their son nail the game-winning shot every night.

Regarding those parents who have, in my opinion, spoken out of turn to me over the years, having been the father of a highschooler myself I can relate to their feelings. You have such a love for your own kid, it's easy to lose perspective. I've seen my son, Tyler, who was in music theater productions and show choir at Athena, get his heart broken when he didn't land certain parts. Did I ache for him? Absolutely. Was I tempted to say something to the director? Yes.

But I don't feel going to that next step is the right thing to do. A parent doesn't really have the background to be able to comment on whether the child deserves the part in a play or to start in basketball. My personal view as a parent is that I'd rather see my son go in and advocate for himself. That teaches him something about taking ownership, and besides, he would understand the feedback better by hearing it directly, rather than having it filtered through me.

The show director and Coach Jim Johnson are not out to hurt Tyler Johnson or any particular player. We've got to do what we, in our position, feel is best. But again, as a parent, it's very hard to accept that there are other kids who are simply deemed more deserving than your child.

In order to better appreciate this reality, it might be wise to cite Reinhold Niebuhr's famous Serenity Prayer: "God grant me the serenity to accept the things I cannot change; courage to change the things I can; and wisdom to know the difference." On the other hand, coaches, players, and parents usually differ on what can and cannot be changed, so that prayer doesn't always work.

Quite often parents envision their son or daughter copping a big college scholarship, and there's extra pressure these days, the way college costs are skyrocketing. But in the great majority of cases, that hope is unrealistic. The thought is, "I'm going to invest in my son's talents by sending him to camps, and someday I expect to reap that investment." The idea is that Johnny's earned his spot on the team simply through the time and expense put in by him and his parents.

But you know what? We coaches are to blame for fueling this mind-set. We've encouraged athletes more and more to specialize in a single sport. Coaches have created a monster by working kids in the off-season, raising the stakes for gaining a competitive edge. It's probably something we can't get out of now. In our Greece Athlete of the Year voting, a hot annual debate is whether a single-sport athlete who's exceptional outranks a three-sport athlete who's simply very good in each sport.

How does all this affect the athletes? Well, I think kids will always be kids—they just want to have fun, not deal with these external pressures. I remember being a child and going outside every day just to *play*, using an old tennis ball or whatever. But organized leagues start at such a young age now. I see a lot less of that impromptu style of recreation, the going out in your yard or to a park and making up games as you go. A lot of children don't know how to play unless it's organized, and that's kind of a shame.

Could the kind of crisis I experienced in December 2005 happen to any team? Absolutely—any sport, male or female, youth league or high school. I was just a bit surprised that after twenty years, I was encountering something so extreme for the first time. Never before in coaching had a dam sprung leaks that I couldn't stop.

Emotionally, I think my rock-bottom point was when all the parents first approached me. For about a week all my stomach did was churn. I had never gotten that feeling for such a length of time. I felt like my insides had been ripped out, and I couldn't get comfortable. I was a nervous wreck, and for the all the motivational books I'd read, all the quotable quotes I'd gathered, I was dumbfounded over this dilemma. The sleepless nights continued.

At first I thought our nine-day layoff between games, from December 3 to December 12, would be good for dealing with the issues and giving us some recovery time. Instead, things became more difficult. I could feel tremendous tension in the air—a lack of peace, a lack of focus. I was carrying a lot of anger and disappointment, but never came out with it to the team or parents. Otherwise, I might have lost control of the whole situation.

We opened our Monroe County Division II schedule with home losses to Irondequoit and Webster Thomas, both league contests. We didn't play with a real passion. Kids were just going through the motions and negativity hung in the air. There was a feeling all around that this team wasn't together, was just full of fragments. We'd had so much adversity, and now it was spreading onto the floor. My thought process had gone from having a championship-contending team to, "Holy mackerel, are we going to put the pieces back together and have a winning season? Are we even going to be able to finish .500?"

Fortunately, Christmas vacation got me away from school and gave me a chance for some quality reflection time. To the players' great credit, they also appeared to be rejuvenated by the break.

A Coach and a Miracle

To a degree, it weighed on my mind who the mastermind was behind the parent revolt. Yet I never did investigate deeply into it, because in some ways I don't want to know. As it was, I had been pretty good friends with a lot of the parents, and the incident did permanent damage to some of those relationships. I lost respect for some of them, even people I'd liked a lot.

Based on all that had happened in December, I couldn't think of a quote of the week much more fitting than the one I selected for the week before Christmas. It's from Norman Vincent Peale's *The Power of Positive Thinking*: "The secret of life isn't what happens to you, but rather what you do with what happens to you."

So what were we going to do with what had happened to us? How were we going to persevere? Well, the basketball schedule wasn't going to wait until we got our internal issues sorted out, so it was time to roll up our sleeves and get back to work.

The Fairport Christmas Tournament was a definite turning point. We had barely won against Lockport in the opening round, while Fairport, a bona fide powerhouse, had beaten Edison—a team we'd needed overtime to beat two weeks earlier—by more than thirty points. As Fairport awaited us in the final, it was one of the first times I ever went into a game thinking we could get massacred. I told my players exactly that in our shoot-around and dared them to prove me wrong. They rose to my challenge by taking Fairport to overtime before losing.

That game brought our mojo back, and we went on a great run the rest of the regular season. After entering the new calendar year with a 4-4 record, we won our next four league games by decisive margins and got a great double-overtime victory at Irondequoit, one of the league's top teams. At that point we were 9-4 overall and 5-2 in the league. The players were mobbing each other after the Irondequoit win; all the parents were hugging the kids; and Kelvin Goff was right in the middle of it. For that

58

particular night, all the turmoil of the past two months was forgotten.

A loss to Webster Thomas snapped our five-game winning streak, but then we won three more in a row. That gave us an 8-3 record in the league, 12-5 overall. As we looked ahead to our regular-season finale against Spencerport, we actually had a chance to tie for the league title with Webster Thomas, which was one game ahead of us and Irondequoit in the standings.

We had been playing much better basketball since the Christmas break. We had successfully switched our defensive approach to a half-court style, and our tri-captains, Levar Goff, Steve Kerr, and Rickey Wallace, were extremely consistent on offense. We started gaining some confidence as everyone became more accepting of their roles.

It was great to see the team persevere and come together. We had finally started playing the kind of ball I knew we could. We'd had some close wins and had also won pretty handily in a lot of games. The players' belief came back, and once it does, that's half the battle. When you go through adversity, you're either going to surrender or become more powerful, and for us it was the latter. The whole team fought past some really trying times—rediscovering its passion for basketball, its mission to be the best team possible, its goal of winning league and sectional titles.

As philosopher William James put it in a quote that I used in late January, "The greatest discovery of my generation is that human beings can alter their lives by altering their attitudes of mind." Luckily, I had enough people like Rickey Wallace who managed to keep their eye on the prize.

"I put all those negative feelings aside because I like to win," Rickey recalled. "When the going gets tough, the tough get going. I tried to pick the team up because I've always been a winner. Losing, that's not a good feeling at all."

Winning doesn't cure all woes, but it certainly mends many. I also sought to maintain team balance by not harping on the past and by remaining positive. Still, it never got back to being completely comfortable for the players, the parents, or me. We'd have weekly pasta dinners and some players would skip them. The controversy changed many relationships within the team, even though Kelvin's name never came up. It was kind of like the elephant in the room.

I never had any direct run-ins with players. But there was a distance, especially with Levar Goff, which was hard because he and I had always gotten along so well.

The parent problems never really subsided, either. It was like opening Pandora's box. As the season progressed, parents came to me frequently about some perceived problem, which almost always boiled down to playing time for their kid.

After trust has been injured and shattered, building it back up can be quite a process. I became much more guarded and stuck to superficial, general conversation. There was that feeling of not knowing whom I could trust anymore. As for Kelvin Goff, my relationship with him remained extremely strained. He would come to all the games and we'd make small talk, but it was certainly no longer the same. And it was obviously difficult for him to be in the same gym with all the other parents.

Through it all, I never stopped being the coach I had set out to be. And I think this fact became evident to the parents, because I still played the kids I thought were going to help us be successful. At some point I think it may have dawned on them that I was playing the Goff boys just the same amount as I did before— even though their father wasn't there beside me during games, supposedly telling me to put his own kids in.

Perseverance is not usually a word that comes up when things are going your way. Often you discover your true ability to persevere only after hitting an extreme low, which was pretty much my situation at the time.

I genuinely believe God threw this adversity in my path so that I'd persevere to become a better person. Nonetheless, all the criticisms stung. Coaches are still human beings, and the daggers thrown at me that season left quite a few nicks.

※

Despite the tensions lingering over our team, J-Mac was having a blast because we were winning a lot. He continued to plow right along, knowing there was a chance he would one day not only get his uniform but maybe even end up playing.

I don't think Jason had complete comprehension of the Goff situation, and in that sense he was a refreshing presence. So much of what I've learned about autism is the need for routine, and J-Mac's adherence to routine was vital for our team at that point. He gave us the perspective that we needed to go back to our own rituals, doing things that had helped us in the past.

"We ended practice every single day by having to make a certain number of free throws, and if a player didn't, he'd have to run sprints. Jason would also shoot, and more often than not he'd swish his free throws," recalled Mike Setzer. "After practice the kids would want to stick around and shoot a little bit—play Horse or do alley-oop passes—and Jason would be right with them. They'd almost always leave with a smile. I do think it helped that Jason was who he was. For a while the kids weren't having fun; Jimmy [Johnson] wasn't having fun. Jason was oblivious. All he wanted to do was win. He did not take sides or show favoritism, so he kind of acted as the glue because he was just for the team."

"If anything, the one word with J-Mac was *encouragement*. I felt like through all those times he was positive. I just think of J-Mac picking us up when we were down," Rickey Wallace added.

I think Jason was one of the few team members whom the Goff brothers felt comfortable around during this stretch. Levar and Kourtney have an older brother who is developmentally disabled, and in that regard I think they've always had a soft spot in their hearts for people like Jason.

Personally, I fed off Jason's excellent attitude while striving to move past this rocky phase. How many people would keep trying out for the team after being cut each year, like he did? How many would stay on as team manager after being so bitterly disappointed, and give every ounce of energy and ability he had? A favorite Bible passage of mine is about the widow donating the two coins. As Jesus observed, she gave all that she had. That's Jason too. He may be limited in certain abilities, but he gives all he has. In light of Jason's perseverance, I guess I really would have been a hypocrite to have bailed out as coach back in December.

One of Jason's single greatest contributions to our team morale was actually quite comical. It came in early December when tensions were near their peak. The team had voted to lighten the mood by going to a nearby Chinese buffet after a Saturday practice. Well, J-Mac put on an eating exhibition like you've never seen. This skinny kid weighing 120 pounds ate for close to two hours straight, consuming amounts that a 320-pounder would have trouble putting away. If everybody could eat like Jason, all those all-you-can-eat places would be out of business. It was incredible. I think it was a combination of Jason being hungry and him doing a little bit for show. Kids would say, "Jason, where are you putting all this?" and he'd go up for another plateful. We all had some laughs together and it was very subtle, but it definitely helped us lighten up at a time when we really needed to.

The internal controversy never changed Jason's goals and thoughts. It was just a bump in the road, and it wasn't going to stop us from achieving his supreme goal—winning sectionals. All he cared about was that we do well on the court, regardless of what happened off the court.

ACTION STEP: *Reflect upon the greatest setbacks in your life, past and present. How did you overcome them, what are you doing to overcome them, or how do you plan to overcome them? How might you handle the breakup of a relationship, the loss of a job, the death of a loved one? Think of other people who have encountered great difficulty due to illness, disability, tragedy, poverty, or discrimination. Study how they persevered despite the long odds they faced. They could be historical figures such as Abraham Lincoln or Martin Luther King, or folks in your own life who have had it worse than you. How did they dig deep to better their situations?*

five

Carpe Diem

Seize the day. This is the culmination of your passion, your mission, your goal setting, your perseverance. When opportunity knocks, are you ready?

AMID THE INCREASED COMPLEXITY OF MY
relationships with many players and parents, I continued to take J-Mac on scouting trips during the season. I never brought up the team controversy and neither did he, even though he was certainly aware of it to some degree. We always kept things light.

As the regular-season schedule wound down, J-Mac was excited for two reasons: The team was winning a lot, and he had his sights very firmly set on wearing that uniform I had promised. He continued to check in regularly with me, as only Jason can, about the uniform's status. Sometimes it seemed like he was asking every day. I'm sure he would have turned the clock forward to the night of February 15 if he could have.

In mid-January, about a month before Senior Night, I set the wheels in motion by asking Josh Harter, head coach at Spencerport High School, what he thought of my idea to put Jason in, since we were playing his Rangers in our final home game. I said, "Look, I want you to be comfortable with this. My intent is not to embarrass your program, but Jason has been so loyal, I really want to give him a senior gift and hopefully get him in the game."

"Jim, I have no problem," he replied. "I know Jason and really think he's a great kid."

I also approached Randy Hutto, our athletic director, and let him know that Jason was physically cleared for action and I had an endorsement from the opposing coach. Being that Randy's own son Joshua is autistic, and that Randy is a pretty compassionate guy in general, he said right away, "My understanding is that he'd be eligible, he'd be fine. I think it's a great idea."

Jason had tried out for the team and had a physical recertification form signed by his parents. He had participated in all the practices, so it wasn't as if we were just plucking him out of the stands. You probably could get into the letter of the law and question whether the practices he took part in really constituted a playing role, but since I had one hundred percent support from the other coach and my athletic director, there was really no issue.

On February 13, two days before Senior Night, Jason went through a full practice with our team for the first time. He was really into it, jumping all over the place with his typical manic energy. I could see at times he was having trouble keeping up with the pace of play up and down the court, but he did get a basket or two. The players were really good with him. They knew about the uniform and the chance that he might play, so their energy level was high. That day I introduced a Ralph Waldo Emerson quote for the week, "Nothing great was ever achieved without enthusiasm," and it fit J-Mac and the rest of our team to a tee.

When practice ended, the long-awaited moment arrived for me to present Jason with his uniform. When I had first approached him with the idea of suiting up, there was no extra uniform available. However, one of our players subsequently quit the team halfway through the season due to lack of playing time.

So, the white-and-gold outfit with number 52 now belonged to Jason. He flashed a big smile, and I could almost hear him thinking, "Oh my God, I got this uniform." Then he turned and left a bit quickly. Maybe he was worried that if he stuck around too long, I'd take the uniform back. I think it's safe to say he floated out of the school building to his father's car. I don't think his feet ever touched the ground.

All the good karma, however, was quickly tempered by another player's unfortunate incident. I had planned to give one of my senior subs, Matt Sheehan, his first varsity start against Spencerport. But that same week, he sprained his ankle badly in physical education class and was unable to play. Instead, he showed up on crutches to be honored for Senior Night along with all the other seniors and their parents.

In a show of support, Steve Kerr wore Matt's uniform, number 4. Steve started the game with four other seniors— Rickey Wallace, Levar Goff, John Swartz, and Rob Tisa. Steve had approached me after school that day and asked if he could wear the jersey in order to boost Matt's spirits. I supported the idea strongly and was able to verify that this was permissible.

It was nice to see both of Levar's parents at the game. I really wasn't surprised that Kelvin showed up, because through thick and thin, he is in it for his kids. There was no question he'd be there, even though it was probably difficult for him.

J-Mac was honored as well, and to see him march out there with that number 52 uniform and headband, then embrace his parents, was really memorable. The national anthem was played and there was Jason, standing closest to the flag as the players lined up along the sideline, his head bowed, just like he had been taking part in pregame rituals for years. This marked the second time in his high school career that J-Mac had dressed for a game, along with two years earlier when he knocked down those three foul shots during the closing moments of the junior varsity season finale.

Although Spencerport was not a big league rival, we had nearly a full house. All season long we had been drawing good crowds, probably the best in my ten years at Athena, thanks in large part to our Sixth Man student section. On top of that, word had started to get out about Jason possibly playing on Senior Night.

Not wanting to take away from the other seniors, I did my best to blend Jason in with the rest of the team rather than single him out. My last pregame statement to the players was, "Let's make it a great night for *all* the seniors."

Since we had beaten Spencerport rather handily in our first meeting, I figured Jason would get into the game at some point. Then again, I wasn't taking anything for granted. Senior Night can be a distraction and I've seen favored teams lose in those situations. Plus, we had to win that game in order to have any hope of tying for the league title.

I also couldn't put Jason in the game until the entire roster had played. As badly as I wanted him in there, a coach simply can't pass over any team member just so the manager can play. I've been a benchwarmer at times in my playing past, so I've always had empathy for those last couple of guys on the bench. Plus, I had worked all year trying to restore team chemistry and didn't want to go into the postseason having slighted the subs.

Fairly early in the game I started hearing "J-Mac" chants spilling down from our student section, but for the reasons just cited, Jason was still riding the pine as the fourth quarter began. By then, the "J-Mac" calls had increased in urgency. Looking back, I'm sure the most suspenseful part of the evening once we had a comfortable lead was the wait to see if and when I'd beckon Jason to take the floor.

Finally, about halfway through the period, I felt the time was right. I rose from my chair and said, "J-Mac," and he jumped up. It all happened within a couple of seconds, with no fanfare on my part, nothing different than any other time I send a player in. But judging from the raucous cheers that went up immediately, it was obvious that many eyes had been peeled on our bench for quite a while.

At this point I'll have to rely on the memory of my assistant, Mike Setzer, because that moment impacted me so greatly that I actually blanked out for a bit.

"I couldn't wait any more for Jason to go in; I wanted to see it happen," said Mike. "I started to tell him, 'Jimmy, I think it's time,' and just in the middle of my sentence he got up and called for J-Mac, who almost beelined right for the court without checking in at the scorer's table. I pointed out to Jimmy to look up in the stands, where everybody was waving the pictures of J-Mac, and he sat down immediately. I think the response of the crowd choked Jimmy up right away. That was the quietest I'd ever seen him. Everybody was jumping up and down and screaming, except Jimmy. He was overcome with emotion and at the same time, I think he was relieved that he'd gotten J-Mac in the game."

It's true that the Sixth Man's reaction just blew me away. I was extremely proud of the school, the way it supported this young man with a disability. Sometimes teenagers will latch onto a situation like that because it's kind of cool; there might not be much sincerity attached to it. Yet in this case, I really felt the kids were so heartfelt in their support of Jason that it brought me to tears.

If you were at the game and unaware of these special circumstances, you'd probably wonder why the Athena fans suddenly went nuts during a stoppage in play. For Jason, their reaction was an unforgettable reward for all those nights of practicing at the YMCA, going to summer camps, never letting go of his goal.

"I was very excited. I know how much that meant to J-Mac. I know how hard he worked in practice every day. You hate to see something like that not pay off," Rickey Wallace said.

I was a high school teacher and coach. If you've worked with young people, you know it wasn't an easy decision. It took great courage to put J-Mac in. You were risking a great deal for that young man; his own self-image, his own sense of hope, his own measurement of accomplishment were pitted up against one great opportunity. But it was an opportunity that Jim judged J-Mac had deserved and earned.

—Tom Rinaldi, ESPN reporter

It's a humane, live, living story of great proportion. Every kid grows up dreaming how they want to be "like Mike" (Michael Jordan) or Larry Bird or Dwyane Wade, and Jim gave him a shot at that.

—Jim Baron, head basketball coach, University of Rhode Island

All scholastic and collegiate coaches share a similar mission, to make it a great experience for their players. Because of that, it was really nice to see Jim give J-Mac a chance. I'm not so sure how many coaches would have taken that approach. At the college level there's more pressure to win games, but at the same time, doing something like Jim did is never far from our minds. It's a good thing to do; it sets a good example for all scholastic and collegiate coaches.

—Paul Hewitt, head basketball coach, Georgia Tech

Rickey's brother John, who led Syracuse University to the 1996 NCAA championship game and went on to play for five NBA teams, was in the crowd on February 15 to experience the electric atmosphere firsthand.

"The kid loves basketball more than anything else in life; it supersedes everything. Everyone that night was happy for him because it didn't matter whether he scored, just that he got in the game—because he loves basketball," John emphasized.

History had been made simply by Jason taking the court. But that was nothing compared to the history that was about to follow.

The entire bench jumped up in anticipation as J-Mac launched his first shot, which missed the rim completely. Then came a missed layup, and pangs of doubt began to set in for me. That's when I started pleading with God to see fit in all his goodness to guide Jason toward making one, just one, basket.

Our next possession saw our guard, Terrance McCutchen, lob a pass up-court to Jason. It was becoming obvious that the players' intent was to get the ball to J-Mac at every opportunity.

Jason let one fly from just beyond the three-point arc on the right-hand side, right in front of our bench. Just as had happened on his first two shots, everyone rose in anticipation and there was a slight hush.

This time the ball rattled home, with 3:11 remaining in the game. My prayer had been answered.

The place just exploded. The screams were absolutely deafening; it was mayhem. As soon as Jason scored, he got right back on defense. But he was so pumped up, jumping all around, he practically tackled a Spencerport player who was dribbling by him. After being whistled for the obvious foul, he stuffed his uniform in his mouth and clapped repeatedly near mid-court while the screams continued. I gestured to him to calm down, though I realized it was virtually impossible for him to honor that request.

It didn't take long for J-Mac to strike again. Twenty-five seconds after he hit that historic three-pointer, at the 2:46 mark, he drained a shot from the left side. His foot was on the three-point line, so it only counted as a two-pointer.

A mere sixteen seconds later, he connected again from three-point range, a bomb from the right side. Over a stretch of just forty-one seconds, he had piled up eight points on three consecutive shots.

He then missed a three-pointer and a layup. But just as soon as his scoring outburst seemed to be subsiding, he hit home from three-point land with 1:39, 1:10, and 0:48 remaining in the game—two baskets from the right side and one from the top of the key. That's another nine points in a span of fifty-one seconds. For each basket that went down, the crowd was stoked to a new level of disbelief and insanity, if that were even possible.

Just like that, Jason was up to seventeen points. The student section began pushing down near the floor, ready to storm the court when the final buzzer sounded.

Amid all this commotion J-Mac dutifully played defense, crouching over and slapping his hands on the floor. He gestured and called out instructions to his teammates, just like he'd been the starting point guard all season. He acted like he was the only person in the building who wasn't completely shocked by the turn of events.

What got caught on film wasn't just Jason making baskets. You saw the people in the stands and even the kid shooting [videotape] into it, because the camera jiggled a little. For that moment on tape, everything was right with the world. It was just the way you want the world to be.

—Steve Hartman, *CBS Evening News* reporter

If you look at the spots where he shot from, Jason had an excellent idea of where the three-point line was. Meanwhile, Spencerport players had picked up on the significance of the moment, and even though they played a certain amount of defense against J-Mac, they certainly weren't pressuring him as hard as they could have. Rangers head coach Josh Harter, who one month earlier had agreed to J-Mac playing that night, was very gracious by not double-teaming Jason or calling a time-out to disrupt his flow. There was really only one time all night that Spencerport attempted to "give" a basket to Jason, when its defense parted like the Red Sea so he could make a wide-open layup—and, ironically, he missed it.

Teammates continued going out of their way to pass the ball to Jason. Guys on our bench were jumping up and down like mad every time he scored, hugging and high-fiving each other. The whole gym continued to rock, with even the Spencerport contingent getting caught up in the moment, despite the fact that their team was getting completely blown out. Even during stoppages of play, the place just kept sizzling with excitement.

With about one minute to go, as I remained rooted to my chair in shock, I got a tap on my shoulder—it was J-Mac's mother, Debbie McElwain, in tears. She said, "Coach, this is the nicest gift you could have ever given my son." She then bent down and gave me a kiss on the cheek.

J-Mac missed on two other three-point attempts as the clock wound down, and it looked like the incredible run was over. But we got the ball back with fifteen seconds left, and Brian Benson inbounded to Jason. He dribbled up-court, the only time he dribbled in the backcourt that night. In my speeches, I like to kid J-Mac that he had it easy that night—work off the screens his teammates set for him, catch the ball, and shoot. I also joke that I'm still looking for his first assist, because every time he got his hands on the ball he shot it.

A Coach and a Miracle

With seven seconds to go J-Mac pulled up from NBA range, his longest attempt of the evening. Come on, wasn't this asking too much in trying to script the perfect finish? Hadn't enough mind-boggling things already happened?

Apparently not. The shot hit nothing but net.

Final score: Greece Athena 79, Spencerport 43. Game's high scorer: Jason McElwain, 20 points. All in the final 3:11. The miracle was complete.

As the buzzer went off, Kourtney Goff led the charge of teammates who mobbed Jason near mid-court. It was pleasantly ironic that Kourtney was out ahead of the pack, after he'd been caught in the middle of our early-season problems.

On the game video you can see our security person, Rod Wagner, with his arms spread—a desperate and fruitless effort to try and hold the crowd back. What seemed like hundreds of kids charged straight past him, just like in the final scene of *Rudy*. Even if J-Mac hadn't hit that last basket, they still would have come out.

Probably the most exhilarating scene occurred next, with Jason being completely engulfed in a swarm of humanity. Soon he was getting a victory ride from his teammates, his arms raised high in triumph while he clutched a basketball. What kid doesn't dream of a moment like this? And yet, how many ever get a chance to experience the moment in real life?

I stood off to the side, still stunned, as I had been ever since Jason entered the game. So I don't clearly remember all the events unfolding. Luckily Marcus Luciano, a Greece Athena student who was serving as our videographer that season, had captured the game and subsequent celebration to preserve the miracle that had just occurred.

A couple of scenes are frozen in my mind, beginning with Matt Sheehan, my injured senior, limping onto the court on crutches amid the mad rush. He was bound and determined to greet Jason.

I'll also never forget Jason's mom, so small, bobbing and weaving through the crowd to get to her son. I think of all the challenges that she and her husband, Dave, endured, raising an autistic and learning-disabled boy, and for them to see him rise above his limitations is as great a thrill as they could have in life.

Jason Bunting announced over the PA that J-Mac had racked up twenty points to finish as the game's high scorer, and a new cheer went up. After a few minutes our Sixth Man cheering section coaxed Jason up into the stands and he started signing autographs of his cardboard-cutout face. This went on for fifteen or twenty minutes, and the buzz never really ceased in all that time.

My son Christopher was one of the more rabid members of the Sixth Man group. He called me on the phone and he was all excited, with a different tone in his voice. What you need to know is that he's not a man of many words. "It's unbelievable; J-Mac hit six threes and we stormed the court at the end of the game and hoisted him on our shoulders." To be honest with you, he really was as excited as if he scored the six three-pointers himself. He was giving a reporter's chronicling of what transpired, and he would never usually call me after a game unless it was, "Dad, I need a ride home."

—Scott Pitoniak, Rochester newspaper columnist

Basketball players, cheerleaders, parents, people from Spencerport—they all wanted to be near Jason. I remember seeing a couple of Athena students who would qualify as "at-risk" embracing him. They're not the type who would normally be at a basketball game, but they had likely shown up that night to support J-Mac. What a treat for them.

Mike Setzer stood next to me while people kept coming up and shouting, "Can you believe this?" Mike's comment was, "The scary thing is we don't have to embellish anything."

No, this Hollywood ending didn't need one bit of fiction added to it. My thought was, "This is right out of *Rudy*," which is based on a true story as well. But there was one big difference between the two unlikely heroes. Rudy got his victory ride for having made a single tackle after getting into the final minutes of a University of Notre Dame football game. With J-Mac, you're talking about an autistic kid who didn't just make one stirring play. He made *seven* shots heard round the world.

He shot seven for thirteen from the field, going six for ten from three-point range. Of our twenty-nine points in the fourth quarter, Jason had twenty of them. He was the only Athena player who scored, or even shot, in the game's final four minutes. His six three-pointers in one game were the most ever under my watch, and possibly a school record. I'm almost certain that his twenty points in a quarter is a school record as well. The scorebook page is quite a sight: Our scorekeeper, Cheryl Tisa, ran out of room trying to mark all the baskets Jason scored, with a line of 3's overflowing the fourth-quarter box for his scoring stats.

This was a story that had all the makings of a major inspirational event even if J-Mac hadn't scored, or if he had just nailed a three-pointer and then come right out of the game. But scoring twenty points in the game's last 3:11? A high-school *team* can't score at that pace. Projected over an entire thirty-two-minute game, that's a rate of about two hundred points per game.

It all reminded me of a completely fictitious motion picture. And yet, not one bit of it was made up. In just a few minutes' time this diminutive seventeen-year-old had turned the tables on a lifetime of struggles caused by his autism.

We finally got back to the locker room, and I soon found out that Webster Thomas had just lost, so we ended up tied for the league title with a 9-3 record (13-5 overall). Earning this co-championship had almost been reduced to an afterthought in light of J-Mac's heroics, but we got a little excited all over again. I told the guys how very proud I was of the way they had come together and made a wonderful memory for the seniors. The funny thing is, I hardly got to talk with J-Mac that night because so many people wanted a piece of him as soon as the game ended.

I went to call the score in to the *Democrat and Chronicle.* The reporter was already aware of what had happened, but she misunderstood. She thought Jason had scored *two* points, not twenty. They were in shock at the newspaper too, after I corrected her.

"Jimmy was like, 'Do you think this will make much news?' This is how dumb we were. We thought the local stations would cover it, but that's all," Mike Setzer recalled.

Instead, this would go on to become arguably the biggest sports story ever to originate in Rochester. Looking back, I think once J-Mac got up over ten points, the saga began to take on mythical proportions.

For this book, I've asked numerous people in the world of media, basketball, politics, and entertainment to lend their perspectives on the impact of J-Mac's accomplishment. Across the board, they've expressed awe, which is really remarkable, since they're at the top of their respective professions and probably thought they'd seen it all.

"It would be like playing golf in your mind and shooting a seventy, and then actually doing that your first time on a golf course," said John Calipari, head coach at the University of Kentucky, who called and congratulated me a few days later. "He probably played that game a thousand times in his mind while he was in the gym by himself."

As far as autism expert Temple Grandin is concerned, Coach Calipari wasn't far from the truth. "Here's what I think happened with him. People don't realize that autistic people are always taking in huge amounts of information while watching games," she said. "He was taking in the movements out on the basketball courts and probably had hundreds and hundreds and hundreds of basketball games in his mind and rehearsed them there—'This corner of the court, this worked before.' He probably had it memorized, what he was going to do."

Ms. Grandin's perspective is worth noting—she is the country's leading author on autism from the perspective of being autistic herself. Whereas she was able to make sense of how Jason carried out his feat, many of my fellow coaches were left simply scratching their heads.

"Under the circumstances, that is absolutely off the map. That may never happen again in our lifetime," said Jim Baron, an old friend who is now the head coach at the University of Rhode Island. "He not only lived up to the coach's confidence in him, but he took it to a new level."

"It was a really amazing display for any player. It was shocking. What happened was unbelievable, one of the great stories of the last number of years," said Jim Boeheim, legendary head coach at Syracuse University.

"You know, I know a lot of really good players who have never had that kind of run—I'm saying at all levels. That's just an unbelievable story," said Bill Van Gundy, for whom I once served as assistant at Genesee Community College. And Bill has seen lots of great players—he has two sons who have served as NBA head coaches: Jeff, who went to the NBA finals with the 1999 New York Knicks; and Stan, who has built a powerhouse with the Orlando Magic.

Unlike his boys, Bill Van Gundy achieved his coaching success in the more obscure ranks of junior college basketball. So he was glad that J-Mac's feat happened in a high school setting, bringing attention to athletic programs that rarely get to enjoy the national limelight.

"One of the things I don't like is if people say it's just a little high school game and that's just a high school coach. Man, there are high school coaches as good as anybody at any level," Bill opined. "And to each kid, the game he's playing in is the most important game in the world. Every game's a big game. To think about the success [J-Mac] had in his big game, to me it's great."

Jack McKinney, a former NBA Coach of the Year whom our team met on a 2007 trip to Florida, compared the elation surrounding J-Mac's historic night to his own NBA title win in 1977 as assistant coach with the Portland Trail Blazers. "The highlight of my career was winning a championship, but I'm very serious—it would be tough to pick what was my highlight, that or being so fulfilled watching this young man reach *his* highlight," he said. "No way would you anticipate that. Even when you see it, you have to pinch yourself and wonder if this is really happening."

My longtime friend Paul Hewitt, the head coach at Georgia Tech who coached the 2004 Yellow Jackets to the NCAA title game, said the atmosphere he witnessed on video of J-Mac's shooting spree surpassed any level of excitement during his team's Final Four run. "Every shot he made, you could see the emotions swelling up. And then everybody stormed the court. What we did [in 2004] doesn't even compare to that," he said.

"I'm not sure we'll ever see anything quite like this again," added Mike Lupica, one of the nation's premier sports writers, who later wrote a column on J-Mac's big night for the New York *Daily News*. "I've been very lucky in my life. I was in Lake Placid when the Americans beat the Soviets in 1980, I saw Kirk Gibson's home run [in the 1988 World Series], I saw the Red Sox come back on the Yankees in '04, I saw a ball roll through Bill Buckner's legs in 1986. I've had a ringside seat to so many great things. I wish I had been there to watch Jason in person. That was one I missed."

Mike further noted, "Rollie Massimino gave a wonderful speech before his Villanova team went out and played nearly a perfect game of college basketball and beat Georgetown, which was supposed to walk all over them, in the NCAA basketball final of 1985. I'm paraphrasing here, but what he said to his kids that night was this: 'For one night, you can beat the best team in the world.' For one magical night, Jason was the best high school basketball player anywhere."

Billy Packer, retired longtime color commentator for CBS, weighed Jason's performance against Villanova-Georgetown and another epic NCAA title-game upset, North Carolina State over Houston in 1983—both of which he announced. "From a standpoint of comparing what he actually accomplished, I would say it exceeded Villanova and NC State. Both those teams sent a number of guys on to the NBA, which probably extended the chances of an upset happening," he said. "[J-Mac] is far more unlikely. This was not a McDonald's All-American scoring twenty points. There was no reason to believe it would happen. I can't imagine that anybody who went to the gym that night and watched him shoot said, 'Yeah, I was waiting for that.' It's a rather staggering accomplishment, almost like a movie you wouldn't enjoy because it wasn't realistic. That's how this almost was—you think it would have not made a good movie, because nobody would have believed it."

Billy's NCAA broadcasting partner, Jim Nantz, was equally in awe—even though as CBS's premier sportscaster he has called numerous Super Bowls, Masters golf tournaments, Final Fours, and other top-shelf sporting events. "I was completely engrossed in this story. It was heroic, unexpected. There's nothing I can think of that can compare to it," Jim said. "I've watched that scene so many times, and you don't turn away. Thank goodness someone was there with the video camera."

Another NCAA broadcaster for CBS, studio analyst and *Sports Illustrated* writer Seth Davis, pointed out that the event's

Getting an early start on my basketball career. (Jim Johnson)

I've got the '70s hair look going during my high-school playing days at Greece Arcadia. (Jim Johnson)

An early-season practice in the fall of 2010. Even after thirty years of coaching, I'm still having a blast. (Jay Shelofsky)

J-Mac (pictured at far left), the biggest Greece Athena fan I know, has been back in the fold since 2008 as a volunteer assistant coach. (Jay Shelofsky)

No longer the scrawny 5-foot, 7-inch team manager, Jason as a young adult now stands six feet tall. (Jay Shelofsky)

I've taught and coached at Greece Athena High School since 1996. (Jay Shelofsky)

J-Mac is engulfed by well-wishers after his miracle twenty-point performance. (Jay Shelofsky)

J-Mac becomes an instant hero, landing in the center of the "Sixth Man" cheering section to sign autographs. (Jay Shelofsky)

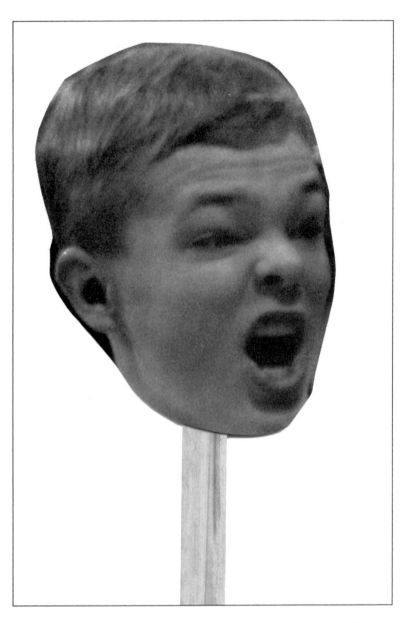

The cardboard cutout of J-Mac's face has now become a collector's item. Athena fans waved hundreds of these placards while cheering him on during his unforgettable varsity debut.

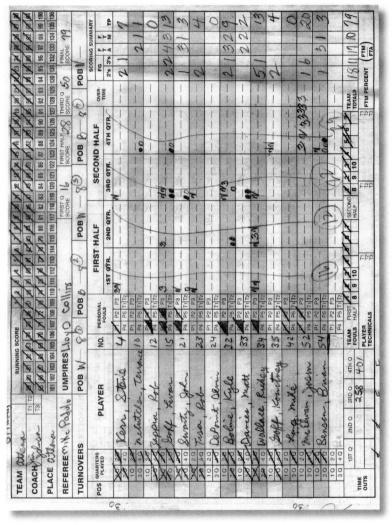

There isn't enough room in the scorebook's fourth-quarter box to log J-Mac's barrage of baskets on February 15, 2006.

J-Mac, my team manager extraordinaire, lends a bit of counsel during the Section 5 final on March 4, 2006. (Jay Shelofsky)

We follow the action during the closely contested sectional title game. (Jay Shelofsky)

Everyone is loving that championship feeling after our 54-51 win over Irondequoit. (Jay Shelofsky)

My family and I celebrate my first sectional title as a coach. From left: My wife, Pat; son, Tyler; mother, Rita; and father, Gene. (Jay Shelofsky)

To James Johnson
With best wishes,

A dream come true: J-Mac, his parents Debbie and Dave, and I meet the President of the United States, George W. Bush. (The White House)

J-Mac, his dad and I enjoy the company of Dick Vitale, ESPN's top basketball personality, during the 2006 Final Four in Indianapolis. (Dave McElwain)

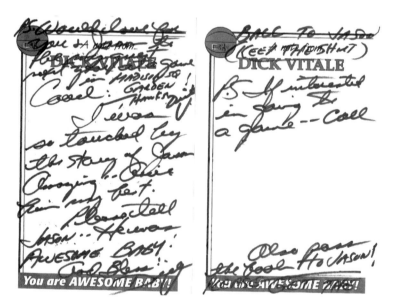

This congratulatory letter from Dick Vitale is among hundreds that I received, from celebrities and non-celebrities alike, after the February 15 game.

J-Mac, Jim Nantz of CBS Sports, J-Mac's dad and I take center court at the Indianapolis RCA Dome before the start of the 2006 Final Four that Jim announced. (Melissa Miller)

I get to appear on the JumboTron at Quicken Loans Arena while our team is honored during a Cleveland Cavaliers game. (Jay Shelofsky)

We enjoy a 2006 meeting with Hillary Clinton, former First Lady and future Secretary of State, while she was serving as a New York State Senator. (New York State United Teachers)

"Magic" is in the air as Earvin Johnson makes a 2006 visit to Greece Athena. (Jay Shelofsky)

I've been appearing behind the microphone quite a bit since the winter of 2006, as audiences never seem to get enough of this miracle story. (Jay Shelofsky)

appeal was greatly enhanced by its occurring in a scholastic setting. "It's the kind of story that could only happen at a youth level. It couldn't happen at the NBA or Final Four level. It takes you back to that time when you first discovered your love of sports," he said.

And of course, no basketball conversation is complete without ESPN's Dick Vitale weighing in. "Well, I think for anybody who had battled adversity, the kid showed incredible courage emotionally and physically. He won the hearts of everyone to be able to make the shots he did. But whether he scored or not, it was still incredible. I think it's a great story—to follow your dream, follow your goals, and never, ever quit. It's a great story for people of my age, people of any age," said Dick, who sent me a lengthy handwritten note of congratulations following the epic night.

Coach Vitale added that a famous quote by his close friend, the late Jim Valvano, sums it all up: "'Don't give up; don't ever give up.' It's a philosophy that applies here, certainly. No question about it."

I've often wondered if, as Temple Grandin suggested, Jason's autism actually enhanced his performance that night. Here's somebody who gets into a game for the first time in front of teammates and peers, misses his first shot by a few feet, and then blows a layup. A lot of other kids would have gone into a shell thinking, "I'm going to be ridiculed for this, be the laughingstock of the school." They'd probably be scared to even shoot again.

But J-Mac just persevered, moving forward. He was bound and determined to get a basket, and wasn't going to let a couple of misses deter him from what he was trying to accomplish.

J-Mac is obviously a gamer, because in the Athena junior varsity's final home game two years earlier, he went three for three from the foul line in a brief amount of playing time. I give Jeff Amoroso, his coach that season, all the credit in the world for providing the model that I eventually followed on the varsity level. It was Jeff who first approached me about the possibility of Jason being the JV team manager. It was also Jeff who sought to get Jason into a JV game.

Jeff was a great assistant for me, and an even better friend. We went through a lot together until he took the varsity job at Victor High in 2004. A strong side of me felt bad that Jeff wasn't part of J-Mac's big night on February 15, because he had paved the way and opened the door in so many ways for Jason. But it didn't take long for Jeff to find out what had transpired that evening.

"I got home late and my wife said, 'Steve Kerr called at eleven. Is something wrong?'" he recalled. "I thought, 'J-Mac must have done something. Jim must have put him in the game.' I went and checked the Section 5 website, and must've done a triple-take when I saw what he'd done. I came back to my wife almost bawling, 'Oh my God, that's why Steve called.'"

Adding to the feel-good nature of this saga was the fact that it involved a great kid with a great personality who had a passion for his team and for the game of basketball. I'm not going to say that everybody loves Jason—he has some traits that annoy people—but he has a basic likability and a big heart, and the student body really rallied around him. These factors make the story so much better.

Most of all, his teammates rallied around him. The most exuberant onlookers during Jason's scoring rampage could be found on the Athena bench, jumping around like lunatics: Matt Sheehan in his street clothes, the Goff brothers, Steve Kerr, Rob Zappia, John Swartz, Rob Tisa, Kyle Boline, Matt Davies, and Rickey Wallace.

An even bigger hats-off goes to the four guys who were on the court with Jason the whole time: Mike Long, Devin DePoint, Terrance McCutchen, and Brian Benson. These were substitutes who rarely got into the scoring column, and they sacrificed their potential points just to give J-Mac more opportunities.

Passing off to Jason was something I had never instruct-ed or even hinted at them to do. As I found out later, it wasn't preplanned on their part, either. They just kind of flowed into the pattern of giving it up for J-Mac.

Brian Benson and Terrance McCutchen, especially, seemed to be looking out for him. Brian had a little more of a personal connection because he lived across the street from Jason and they were friends. During the game he went out of his way to get the ball to J-Mac—for example, grabbing an offensive rebound and instead of going back up with it, kicking it back out to Jason. But I was surprised that Terrance had that same instinct; he's a fairly quiet kid, so quite honestly, I didn't know what he'd do in that situation.

"When J-Mac got in the game, shooting was not on my mind. It wasn't on anybody's mind; it was just in our hearts so strong to let him have as much fun as he wanted. But I didn't think he was going to have *that* much fun," Terrance said. "Passing to him, it just came from the heart. Nobody talked about that ahead of time. It was his day."

All the life lessons I've tried to teach in my career came out that night, even though we'd been so fragmented two months earlier. Maybe somehow, some way, all those quotes and themes about teamwork actually sank in as the season went on. You don't always know if your message is getting through, especially to a bunch of teenage boys, but the essence of teamwork was on display on February 15. It was such a great feeling to see the team come together the way it did.

I learned a lesson or two of my own that night about the value of perseverance and staying focused on my mission and goals. Had people encouraged me to follow through on my temptation to resign early in the season, I never would have witnessed this once-in-a-lifetime scoring exhibition.

For anyone who was there, what unfolded in the Greece Athena gym defied any logical explanation. That's why I'm certain that a real miracle occurred right before my eyes. And I'm not the only one who believed that the good Lord was presiding over the festivities that night.

"It was a gutsy move—you never knew what was going to come out of it. You didn't want a moment of condescending glory. You wanted something where J-Mac and his family felt good," said George Pataki, then the governor of New York state, who would welcome J-Mac and me to Albany later that spring. "The outcome was tremendous; it was just terrific. It makes you wonder if the hand of God wasn't helping with the direction of that ball just a little bit."

"Obviously, nobody ever believed he could do it," said Jeff Van Gundy, a longtime friend who is now a top NBA broadcaster. "It makes you believe more strongly in the human spirit and that there's a greater being out there than human. I don't want to sound like a real religious person, because I'm not, but there was definitely something there that night."

At least two of my players also believed in the miracle aspect of what they had witnessed.

"It was just a blessing, something so sacred. That gym was trying to say something," Rickey Wallace remarked. "It's just a blessing from God, the fact that Coach Johnson had it in himself to put J-Mac in the game and that he hit those shots."

"I say, God just held J-Mac back because he had autism and then told him, 'Well, I'm gonna make up for that and give you the best year of your life,'" Terrance McCutchen said.

I've now seen the game video hundreds of times and still get choked up. It was a complete celebration of humanity, starting in the Athena gym and spreading all over the world as the story quickly gained attention.

Jason's dream came true, and I love that I played a role in that happening. I hadn't been looking to get any publicity; I just wanted to do something for a fine young man. I felt that God rewarded the situation because it was done for the right reasons. It was his special way of saying, "Jim, what you're doing as a coach and as a person is right." He allowed me to go from my all-time nadir in coaching to my all-time high in a period of just a couple of months.

As Jason has said many times in interviews, the atmosphere at Greece Athena that night was like we'd won the NCAA championship. It is remarkable that such excitement could be generated from what wasn't even a playoff game.

Our postseason actually was just about to begin—and there were still plenty of thrills in store.

ACTION STEP: *Decide right now something you want to pursue, and spend at least fifteen minutes daily working toward it—reading, listening to a cassette, watching a video, picking the brain of a mentor, practicing. Are you spending time each day on improving yourself? Are you growing your skills? Are you growing as a person? J-Mac didn't know if he was ever going to get into a game, but he was ready when his moment arrived—not just to play, but to shine. You never know when your time is going to come. You may be only a single step from attaining your dream. What are you doing today to prepare for your opportunity?*

six

Be a Team Player

Do your individual goals also promote the betterment of others?

WHEN I FINALLY GOT HOME VERY LATE ON THE
night of February 15, Pat and Tyler were still up after having
attended the game together. They were just as blown away as I
was; my wife said that during J-Mac's scoring barrage she kept
yelling, "Oh my God, oh my God!" I lay awake for quite a while,
in heaven on earth, thinking, "Wow."

The next morning our family went through its usual routine,
although I was a bit anxious to grab the daily newspaper to see
Jason's name in bold type. Instead, the headline simply read,
THREE TEAMS SHARE DIVISION II CROWN, with us being one of
those teams. Farther down a brief mention was made of Jason's
accomplishment, but it certainly didn't command the space I'd
thought it would.

But then I got to school and there was a buzz everywhere. I
put the news of Jason's feat in the morning announcements, and
kids started coming down to the athletic department wanting to
see the videotape. Tears were streaming down the cheeks of both

male and female students, and lots of them were asking to watch it again. I probably showed the last four minutes of the game at least ten times, and didn't end up teaching a whole lot that day. The kids were saying, "Coach, this is unbelievable. It's going to be on ESPN." My reaction was, "ESPN? It doesn't even get a headline in the local paper!"

It wasn't until I watched the tape that I got a clear sense of how J-Mac's teammates had reacted to his scoring binge, how they were going so crazy on the bench. Watching that and the fans' reaction in detail was a very touching experience, seeing how happy everyone was for him. The funny thing is, all you could ever see of me was my back, since our videographer, Marcus Luciano, was in the stands behind our bench. And the only time I ever really moved on tape was when I got up to signal Jason into the game.

To me, Marcus captured that event as well as any professional cameraperson. Despite using very average equipment, he did a phenomenal job of getting all Jason's baskets and scanning the crowd for its reaction whenever Spencerport had the ball. Normally you'd film the opposing team's possessions, but Marcus got the real story by zooming in on the fan response. I was impressed that he had such instincts, because it was only his third or fourth time doing game video for us. He also kept the camera running long after the game ended, so as to preserve every moment of this once-in-a-lifetime celebration.

Unbeknownst to me, Andy McCormack, Jason's speech/language pathologist, had already alerted a local television station, WROC, about the video and they agreed to pick up the tape.

Andy seemed to have a pretty good inkling of the weight J-Mac's feat would carry in public, so he not only tipped off the media but also prepped Jason on his impending celebrity status. "I would say I was pretty close with him, so the day after the game I pulled Jason aside and told him, 'Your life is about to

change; you're going to become famous. People are going to try
to be your friends. People are going to look for opportunities.
Just remember who your friends were before this all happened,'"
Andy said.

WROC ran our game highlights on that evening's newscast. Sports director John Kucko led into the segment by saying,
"Something happened last night in Section 5 which is gaining
fast attention."

Indeed it was. The next afternoon, February 17, interview
crews came to Athena at practice time. Jason, his mother, and I
were interviewed by WROC, WHAM, and R News 9 for stories
that all aired that night. The three most frequently shown clips
were of me putting Jason in the game and players and fans starting to cheer; him making his first basket and the crowd letting
out an ear-splitting scream; and the game ending and everyone
rushing the floor.

At about eight o'clock in the evening, I got a call from Mike
Catalana, sports director at WHAM. He said, "Jim, this story is
unbelievable. Would you mind if I sent it out nationally?" So he
forwarded it to CNN, which became the first national network
to air our game highlights.

"I couldn't wait to get out to the school to interview Jason, and
I couldn't wait to get it on air that day," Mike recalled. "When
the story first aired, phones started ringing—'Can you show that
again?' That's when we sent it to CNN, and ABC had it on the
news feed for any local affiliate. It ran all over the country; it just
exploded. I've certainly never had a story with even remotely that
kind of reach."

Another local journalist, Scott Pitoniak, then of the *Democrat and Chronicle,* has also used the word *exploded* in describing
the story's ascent. As for me, that weekend was actually pretty
quiet; I got only one media call. The climb from a big local story
to a huge national story had begun but I still didn't foresee it,

since the memory of our local newspaper giving the event a small write-up was still etched on my brain.

On Monday, February 20, we had a morning practice because the school had begun winter recess. My theme was "team and togetherness," and I plugged in the Archibald Rutledge quote "One of the sanest, surest, and most generous joys of life comes from being happy over the good fortune of others."

I got a sense the story was building when CBS—which had acquired the game video from John Kucko at WROC, its affiliate in Rochester—got in touch to send a crew to Greece for a national feature. Then CNN did a live interview with Jason and me from the R News 9 studio in Rochester on Thursday, February 23. I drove Jason to the studio and said, "J-Mac, do you believe this is happening?" He said, "No, Coach," but otherwise our conversation, as usual, revolved around basketball.

The CNN interview was not terribly smooth. Jason was just all over the place answering questions and running at the mouth, and I felt uncomfortable for both him and myself, because I didn't think I did a good job either. It's pretty intimidating to do a live national interview for the first time, because you know there's no option of editing out the parts where you stumble.

I felt a lot better that evening when *CBS Evening News* closed out its broadcast with an excellent documentary-type segment that included interviews with J-Mac and me. Anchorman Bob Schieffer introduced the piece, and this one was very special because it was the first to address the story behind the story. Reporter Steve Hartman, who had come to one of our practices, delved into the struggles Jason had faced in his life. After the piece finished, with the crowd lifting J-Mac high in triumph, Schieffer paused a few seconds before saying in a hoarse voice, "That's just great," and signing off. Not only did the feature evoke visible emotion from him, but the audience response was so staggering that CBS actually reran the piece the next night.

"It was a thrill covering this," Hartman said. "We talked about doing a follow-up and then the president of CBS News, Sean McManus, said, 'Let's rerun the story.' That's kind of outside the box for us and everybody was taken aback, but then they said, 'Why not?' We were flooded with phone calls and e-mails. The late, great Ed Bradley was actually hosting the news that next night. He mentioned that it was the first time in his thirty years at CBS that it had ever been done, airing the same story on back-to-back nights."

In between the two straight nights with the CBS feature, we had a Friday-morning sit-down with no less than three national outlets for live interviews: ABC's *Good Morning America,* CNN's *American Morning,* and ESPN2's *Cold Pizza.* Only one week earlier, that same gym had accommodated three local stations, and now here were three national media powerhouses. By this point I had started to send out quite a few tapes of our game highlights, using a VCR at our school to make copies.

ABC's Charles Gibson asked Jason, "How are you usually on three-pointers?" and Jason replied, "Not as good as this, I can tell you that," which set off laughs from everyone. The lead-in to CNN's story was accompanied by John Fogerty's song "Center-field" and its famous refrain, "Put me in Coach, I'm ready to play," and interviewer Soledad O'Brien mentioned on the air that she has an autistic nephew. Meanwhile, ESPN stayed for a good deal of the afternoon filming a documentary piece that came out two days later.

By then the story was on its way to becoming an Internet sensation as well.

"I know in the weeks following the first J-Mac feature there were more video web hits on ESPN.com than any other piece of video up to that point in time. It was more than a million, and it's just amazing to think that," said Dan Arruda, who produced two J-Mac–related stories for ESPN.

My wife was watching SportsCenter and she asked if I'd seen the incredible performance by the high school kid who was autistic. I said no, and she said, "Well, you've got to see this." I never did see it that night. Another day goes by and all of a sudden I'm watching SportsCenter and I can't believe my eyes. I've seen great basketball players the last forty years and a lot of great performances, but I've never seen anyone at any level— elementary school, high school, college, pros—perform like that for that period of time. I yelled to my wife and she said, "That's what I was trying to tell you about!"

—Jim Larranaga, head basketball coach, George Mason University

I couldn't wait to tell this story to my players [who were ranked in the country's top five for much of the 2005–06 season]. It would show them the impact that an opportunity for J-Mac had, that just getting into one game meant the world to him and that we should all appreciate the opportunity we have and be humbled, not get out of touch with reality because of our success.

—Jay Wright, head basketball coach, Villanova University

Jason and I were now both getting more comfortable with the interview process, with Jason flashing his innocent smile much more regularly. It helped that a lot of the same questions kept coming up and we could be more prepared with our thoughts. During the interviews Jason started using some lines that would surface in many subsequent interviews: "I was shooting three-pointers like free throws." "The basket was like a huge bucket." "I was hotter than a pistol."

Jason was developing quite a rapport with reporters, and I gave him a few interviewing tips, which added another nice dimension to our relationship. I also made sure to include some team members in our interviews, which helped make them feel a part of things.

With school on a one-week break that week, a lot of media calls went to my house, although I don't know how people had gotten my phone number. I came home one day and my wife was distraught. She literally threw two pieces of paper at me with close to a hundred messages, said, "I'm not your secretary," and ran out of the house. Pat is very supportive of me in all phases of my coaching, but it just goes to show how intense the pressure became.

On Saturday morning, February 25, we had a team shoot-around with no media; our first sectional game was that night. We also chatted for a bit, and I mentioned that it was important to have our minds on the game but also to embrace the extra attention, because it was a real opportunity for our program to shine. Jason gave a little pep talk of his own, along the lines of, "This is what we played for, so we've gotta stay focused." He was worried about the players losing focus because of the attention he had attracted, to the point that he seemed to feel a little guilty about it.

"Stay focused" was fast becoming his catchphrase, and it was always in the context of wanting the team to stay focused on its collective goal rather than individual goals. J-Mac was absolutely remarkable in that he remained a team man through and through. Even in his interviews with national media, he went out of his way to say how happy he was that the team was doing well.

After receiving a first-round bye we had our first sectional playoff game that evening, a home contest against Greece Arcadia, my alma mater. We were the No. 2 seed in the Section 5 Class AA tournament.

There were probably a few rumors floating around that Jason was going to be in the game, and I can understand why people would draw that conclusion. But the truth is that adding him to our roster again was not even an option. First of all, sectional rules state that a player has to play in a minimum of six regular-season games in order to compete in a playoff game, unless the reason he wasn't playing was injury related.

Besides, the bubble would surely have burst, because Jason was never going to duplicate that twenty-point feat against the kind of competition he'd be facing. I've seen Jason play plenty, and it wasn't that I felt I'd misjudged his abilities. He could shoot quite capably, but dribbling, passing, handling pressure from opponents, playing defense, his small size, and his inability to jump high were all areas that kept him from being a varsity-level player.

Finally, having Jason play wouldn't have been fair to all the other guys I had cut along with him in preseason. The Spencer-port game was really a one-time deal, a gift for all his dedication, and he understood that. There was never from Jason, "Coach, I scored all these points, so I should play." Whatever was best for the team was fine with him.

To me, this speaks to all the great things sports can teach about unselfishness, caring about your team, and being a good teammate. For that kid to accept being back in the role of a manager . . . People are going to focus more on the miraculous twenty points than everything else, but what makes it a story is all the other factors. There's a lot J-Mac can teach our kids too.

—Jeff Van Gundy, former NBA head coach and current NBA television analyst

---

We coasted to a 66-42 victory over Arcadia, never really being threatened. We had a full house on our home court, where we were playing for the first time since history had been made there ten nights earlier.

Obviously, some people were on hand due to the media stuff that had been building. CBS wanted to mike Jason for a future feature, so we had a humongous microphone over our bench for the game. It takes a lot to subdue J-Mac, but he didn't know what to make of that microphone and sat rather quietly next to Mike Setzer most of the night.

For me, the win was a big relief. Not only had we been dealt a number of recent distractions, but we had lost heartbreakers to Arcadia in the sectional semifinals each of the previous two years. So it was good to have this game behind us.

J-Mac and I went into a separate room after the game and were interviewed for *People* magazine, and nationally renowned columnist Mike Lupica called me that night. So the media attention kept rolling right along.

The next day, an excellent ESPN documentary came out. My comments were featured extensively, and by the end of the piece I was obviously getting choked up on television. Dan Arruda, the producer, had asked me some powerful questions about the significance of J-Mac's performance, and even though I had tried to tell myself not to cry on national TV, I couldn't hold back. And yes, I cried all over again when I watched the feature for the first time. The entire five-minute package was so well done, with Tom Rinaldi providing terrific narration.

I got only one call that Sunday and figured things were dying down. Then it was back to school the next day, following a one-week break. I was given the option of having a substitute for my physical education classes, but I figured I'd be fine.

Boy, was I wrong. Not in my wildest dreams did I ever expect what happened. The messages had stacked up because of the week's layoff, and once people realized school was open, the phone started ringing incessantly.

A Coach and a Miracle

The athletic director's secretary, Ann Marie Paul, took to making several lists of people who had left messages. Here and there I'd try to find some quiet place for an hour, and would come back to find ten more voice mails. My colleagues in my physical education office tried to take messages, but they didn't stand a chance of keeping up the pace. E-mails were piling up rapidly too, and it didn't help that I was not a frequent user of e-mail. Luckily I had my basketball scorekeeper, Cheryl Tisa, the mom of one of the players, helping me go through all the electronic messages.

Whether at home or at school, the messages were always related to the miracle game: congratulations, movie offers from studios both big and small, media requests, you name it. I was on so many radio sports talk shows and interviewed by so many daily newspapers. The New York Mets wanted Jason and me to come to their home opener.

Many of the calls were from people desperately trying to reach Jason, whose home phone number was unlisted, so I was the guy doing the majority of the contacts. They were all wonderful opportunities, but unfortunately some of them went by the wayside because there simply wasn't enough time. We were big-time celebrities, and there was no escaping it. Almost all the time I was exhausted, yet wired. It was both stressful and exhilarating.

I try to be gracious to everybody and in general strive to return messages within twenty-four hours. Unfortunately that policy went right out the window. I began to appreciate how difficult it is for celebrities who always have media attention, which I had previously known nothing about. At the high school level, if you get a camera to come to your practice it's a big deal. Now I was getting five camera crews per day—even one from Japan.

Hong Kong, England, Germany, Spain, Australia, Japan— these are just a few of the places around the world that carried our game video on their TV stations and/or ran articles about

Greece Athena in their newspapers. All in all, the video eventually got millions of hits on ESPN.com and YouTube, and lives on today thanks to the miracle of cyberspace.

For eight days I had to use a sub for my physical education classes, even though I was at the school. It was all I could do to keep up with practice and preparation for the next sectional game.

That first day back to school was perhaps the most insane in terms of the impact and attention J-Mac's feat had garnered. But there was very little time to waste, since we were facing McQuaid Jesuit in the sectional semifinals the very next night. Here was another chance to go to my first sectional final ever, and I was smack in the middle of perhaps the most stirring sports story ever to hit Rochester. But the media would have to wait, because I could not allow even a story of this magnitude to come between me and the team.

Approximately six thousand people turned out the next night, February 28, to Blue Cross Arena in downtown Rochester—also known as the Big House in Section 5 circles. That's about twice as many fans as you'd normally get for a game of that importance.

We played stellar defense all night long and led by ten points at halftime, but McQuaid took the lead with approximately six minutes to go in the game. Having lost all six of my previous sectional semifinals—including three or four in the final minute—I started to have flashbacks and feel the skeletons coming out of the closet.

But I just said to myself, "Jim, you've got to stay focused on the matter at hand. This is not going to happen again." *Stay focused, stay focused.* Now even I was feeding off the power of J-Mac, incorporating his pet phrase when I needed it the most.

We rallied mightily down the stretch for a 52-41 win to advance to the championship game. Rickey Wallace was our top scorer, with sixteen points, which came as no surprise. But our other two captains, Levar Goff and Steve Kerr, had seven and eight points respectively, even though they were almost locks for reaching double figures every night. Instead we got great performances from Kyle Boline, a junior forward, with fourteen points, and Brian Benson, our quickly emerging sophomore center, with seven points, seven rebounds, and four blocks.

It's often inexplicable why badly needed clutch performances come from the people you least expect. All I can think of is that once again the power of J-Mac had struck and Kyle and Brian were doing their own impressions of him. Maybe they started saying to themselves, "Wow, if J-Mac can do it, there's an opportunity for all of us." It's just one of many ways the night of February 15 put our entire team on a completely different plane.

As for me, it was a great relief to finally get to a sectional final. I think my kids really knew it too. They hugged me and said, "We did it for you, Coach."

The next day, March 1, I was a guest on Jim Rome's ESPN radio show and ended up doing a twenty-minute interview with him. He had to bump his other guests because he was so enraptured with our story and had so many people calling in.

Jim Rome has a reputation for hitting some raw nerves and not being afraid to ask the tough questions. So I wasn't sure what approach he would take with me, since I was already getting some kidding from people in the media—for instance, Charles Barkley said I should be fired for not having played J-Mac until the regular season's final game. But Rome ended up being very sincere with me; I think the story touched him deeply.

That night I was watching a sectional game with my friend Chris Cardon, whose Irondequoit team we would face in the Class AA title game. I told him I had to leave Blue Cross Arena a bit early because Magic Johnson was calling my house at ten o'clock. He thought I was kidding: "Magic Johnson is calling your house?" And I said, "Yeah, I can't believe it, either."

Magic Johnson indeed called me from Hawaii that night. He wanted to be involved with the production of a movie about Jason's life, and my character would have a featured part as well. We talked for about fifteen minutes. It was exciting, and I was a little nervous, thinking, "Is this really Magic Johnson?"

The next two days were mostly fun. Another CBS feature with Steve Hartman, spotlighting Greece Athena's special-education unit, of which Jason was a part, made its debut. J-Mac attended a finalists' brunch along with me and his fellow seniors. He was singled out by Mike Catalana, of WHAM, who served as emcee. "Anybody stand up who's ever scored a point in a varsity basketball game," Mike instructed the room, before adding, "and remain standing if you scored twenty points in your first game." J-Mac had a huge smile as he, naturally, was the only one to remain on his feet. Later that day he visited a class at Pinebrook Elementary School in Greece.

The players were hanging close to Jason during all the media fanfare. I think it's natural for all people, especially kids, to think, "Jeez, I want to be on TV." And at that point, the way to do it was to be around Jason. They knew the camera was running. I made sure I rotated different players to be interviewed so no one would feel slighted. It was potentially very touchy.

But I really don't think the players were ever jealous of the exposure J-Mac got. I think a lot of it had to do with him keeping his ego well in check and never abandoning his team-first attitude, which only strengthened the love and admiration his teammates had for him. His reminder to stay focused was very helpful for all of us, and that mantra just grew and grew the deeper we went into the playoffs. In fact, I remember being interviewed by a local television station at Blue Cross Arena prior to our championship game. They asked if they could interview Jason as well, and since there was still plenty of time before the game began, I asked him about it. His reply: "Coach,

I can't right now. It's too close to the game and I've got to get focused."

The only negative part of our climb to the championship game was one of our recurring themes from the 2005–06 season: parents wondering why their kids weren't playing more. One mother approached me the day after the McQuaid win because her son, a substitute, hadn't played at all in that game. Then I made a starting lineup switch going into the sectional final, and that set off a whole new tiff, with the dad of another player. It's ironic, because I'd begun getting these touching e-mails and phone calls from friends and strangers for the role I had played in Jason's saga. The messages would say what a big heart I have, what a nice guy I am. But some of my players' parents were indicating much different feelings toward me.

You might have figured that some of that conflict would subside because our team was playing so well, but no. I call it the "big-win syndrome," because I've seen it happen before. Maybe God does this to keep things in perspective. It's uncanny. After some really big win, something happens involving a player who wasn't getting his desired amount of playing time or enough balls passed his way. And you think to yourself, "We're playing so well. Is this really a good time to air these grievances?" But I suppose the bigger the game, the more individual jealousies can come to the surface. That's why it was so refreshing to have a fellow like J-Mac around, who was about the team and nothing else. On the other hand, as much as his positive influence rubbed off on lots of folks, it didn't reach everybody.

All the controversy took a backseat when Saturday evening, March 4, rolled around, as we took the Blue Cross Arena floor against Irondequoit for the Section 5 crown. It wasn't going to be easy. The Eagles were the top seed and we had split two close games with them during the regular season.

Attendance was huge that night—some ten thousand people, the biggest crowd I'd ever encountered while playing or coaching. Of course, a lot of it had to do with the attention Jason was getting. Many folks were there simply to get a glimpse of him, even though he was back in his customary dress shirt and tie and not playing. A local company had made up a bunch of J-Mac T-shirts with the words STAY FOCUSED; they were all over the arena.

It was a pretty "wow" moment. ESPN even showed highlights from the game later. In a lot of respects the atmosphere seemed more like an NCAA championship game.

What also helped was the long tradition of importance our city has placed on the Section 5 tournament. The pinnacle for a lot of schools around Rochester is to get to the Big House and win that sectional, and whatever happens in the state tournament is anticlimactic. I think we have about the best-operated sectional tournament in the state, and I'm proud to say that my dad, Gene, helped maintain that degree of excellence as the former Section 5 and state basketball chairman. Our sectional games are very well attended. They may not equal an Indiana state championship with twenty-five thousand people, but the tournament is still very special.

Adding to the tournament's importance is the fact that Rochester, while a big enough city to have a number of professional sports teams, is just a rung below the major leagues in terms of size. And although we're less than one hundred miles down the New York State Thruway from the Orange of Syracuse University, we don't have a college Division I basketball program of our own. So, I think the focus becomes stronger on our metropolitan area's high school basketball playoffs.

This marked Athena's first appearance in a sectional final since the Trojans had won in 1992 behind Rickey Wallace's brother, John, and gone on to earn the state public high school title. As for me, it was the first time I'd been on the bench and not in the stands for a championship game. We were going up against an excellent Irondequoit team being coached by my close friend, Chris Cardon, who, like me, was a veteran coach still looking for his first sectional trophy.

Irondequoit went up 13-2 in the game's opening minutes and led 16-7 after one quarter, so the prospect for the Hollywood ending that people across the country had come to expect wasn't looking good. Jason, in a white dress shirt and gold tie, was beside himself with anxiety, slapping the floor, grabbing his head, and waving his arms every which way. Even though there were numerous cameras on him, none of his actions were for show. He was in complete agony that his team was getting shelled.

To Irondequoit's credit, the team made four three-point baskets in the first quarter, a couple of which were real bombs. Our own players appeared a bit shell-shocked at some of those early shots, and they were probably very nervous playing in front of a packed house with so much media attention. These are still kids, and you can hope but not necessarily expect that they won't be affected by the immense pressure.

Our early deficit was a litmus test for me, and I managed to stay calm in the face of the storm. That wasn't always Jim Johnson. At points during narrow sectional losses in the past, I hadn't done a very good job of keeping my emotions in check when the pressure was on. My players in turn would feel the heat—and who knows to what degree a key turnover or forced shot might have been connected to that?

This time I simply reassured the kids, and myself, that Irondequoit couldn't keep up its pace with its three-point shooting. We switched to a triangle-and-two defense, which helped start turning the tide. We fought back to 27-23 by halftime and it was nip and tuck throughout the second half.

With slightly more than two minutes remaining, we held a five-point lead over the Eagles. But since nothing had ever come easily in these situations during my coaching past, it seemed fitting that we committed a couple of turnovers and Irondequoit tied the score by nailing a three-point basket and a couple of free throws. By this point J-Mac's white dress shirt was half out as he continued to flop around in distress like a fish.

We got the ball with forty seconds to go and the score tied at 51. I opted not to take a time-out, feeling that we should be well enough prepared to run the correct play. The players patiently passed and looked for an open shot. Finally Levar Goff sought to take charge by driving down the right side, but he got trapped too far under the basket, with no place to go.

He had the presence of mind to kick the ball out to Steve Kerr, who launched a three-point attempt with thirteen seconds left; it hit nothing but net. I remember feeling a sense of relief amid the bedlam, thinking, "Oh my God, somebody's finally made that shot"—the clutch shot that had never gone my way in past sectional tournaments. Steve's basket enabled him to finish as the game's high scorer, with nineteen points, including eight in the final quarter.

Irondequoit called time-out and then missed a long three-point try. There was a scramble for the rebound and the Eagles tried a desperation three-pointer that was way off the mark. The game and sectional title belonged to our Trojans, 54-51.

I'd barely even heard the buzzer when I was tackled by Mike Setzer. On the court, J-Mac went back up on the players' shoulders, just like he had on February 15 after his twenty-point game. Here was a night he didn't even play, but somehow he still emerged as the hero.

It wasn't long before the players started running toward our exuberant fans in the stands. In fact, Steve Kerr jumped right over the wall and into the seats, and started hugging some Athena students with disabilities more severe than Jason's. I hadn't realized that Steve had begun to work pretty extensively with this group of young people, volunteering his time every week.

Jason was jumping up and down in his typical disheveled state, thrusting his fingers in the air and making the "No. 1" sign toward the delirious Athena crowd, which, truthfully, had their eyes more on him than on any player. A few moments later, Steve began straightening out Jason's shirt and tie, making him look spiffy for the cameras.

And there were plenty of cameras. After the trophy presentation Jason and I were both deluged by media, a now rather commonplace occurrence. But I was torn because I didn't want the night to be all about Jason and me, since neither one of us had even played.

In the locker room I told all the players how proud I was, that they had shown such great resilience through all the distractions that had popped up in 2005–06, that what they had done would be embedded in my heart and memory forever. Then I joined in with my troops for some crazy dancing around the locker room.

We had finally done it. We had fulfilled the hopes and maybe even expectations of people across the country who had first heard of our team through J-Mac's story.

As much as I value the team above individual achievement, I most certainly took satisfaction in finally getting my first sectional title. I think all coaches would be lying if they said it wasn't important to win a championship of significance. For instance, Jim Boeheim has been ridiculously successful as Syracuse University's head coach since the late 1970s, but it wasn't until his first national championship, in 2003, that many people gave him complete validation.

Would I have gotten that monkey off my back without all that happened with J-Mac? I tend to think not. To me, his big night on February 15 united our team at a new level. I will never forget that the substitutes passed off to Jason every chance they got, without even a mild suggestion from me to do so.

Take a guy like Terrance McCutchen. He was a junior guard who had a hard time being relegated to the bench after playing regularly on the junior varsity the year before. But all that he cared about on February 15 was making sure that Jason had a chance to shine.

Then there were my players' reactions from the bench as Jason lit up the place. For every shot he took they rose to their feet in anticipation. For every one that fell, they jumped and screamed, exchanging hugs and high fives. It couldn't have mattered less at that point that parents were disgruntled with my coaching decisions, or that we'd almost had a mutiny when the season began.

Along the lines of team support, our Greece Athena fans also deserve major credit for the way they rallied around Jason, waving blow-up photos of him, urging me to put him in the game, not getting down on him when he missed his first couple of shots, storming the floor when the game ended.

My players continued to put teamwork first during the postseason. We had fourth-quarter deficits in the semifinal and championship games, but maintained our composure and won them both. There was just that inner desire. No matter what distractions existed during the season, we got through them together. There's a lot of truth to the saying that adversity either tears you apart or makes you stronger. J-Mac may have commanded a lot of the headlines, but I loved all the guys in the 2005–06 club because they were truly team players.

Is it possible that all those life lessons I had preached during the season had taken hold? There's no measurable way of knowing, but I am very sure that I emphasized teamwork every day, all year long, and it sure showed up at the end. What I also know is that selflessness, not selfishness, on everybody's part allowed us to enjoy our biggest successes in 2005–06. There were so many compelling examples of the importance of placing others first, even as individual goals are being pursued or realized.

And, of course, there was Jason. Right as he was becoming a huge celebrity, he graciously and willingly went back to being team manager. In interviews afterward, he said he was happier about getting a sectional title in his senior season than about scoring twenty points in his only varsity game.

The win made me think back to arguably my most disappointing loss ever, when we were knocked out of sectionals in 2003–04 by a close semifinal loss to Greece Arcadia. I'd thought we had the game won, and then Arcadia started making crazy shots while we came up empty in clutch situations. Once again the door had been slammed shut on my chances of reaching a sectional final. That was the game that caused me to go home and completely lose my temper, more so than at any other time in my life. It caused me to rant toward my wife in language she's not used to hearing.

A few days later I was talking to my mother, still down in the dumps. She said, "I know you're upset, but Jim, something just tells me God has something better for you. God has got a better plan."

I wasn't so sure. Wouldn't you know it, almost the exact same thing happened the next year—a close loss to Arcadia in the sectional semifinals. Once again I was devastated, and then the following season began with the massive team controversy that pushed me to the brink of resigning. How was this supposed to be a part of God's better plan?

As it turned out, my mom was a prophet. I went from the low of my coaching career to its extreme high in less than one season, only deepening my belief that this was all connected to a miracle. Interestingly, the sectional title, which I had coveted so long, turned out to be only part of an even greater saga.

I believe the chief purpose of a miracle is to impact and inspire other people. In that regard, the journey for J-Mac and me was just beginning. I still find it unfathomable how incredibly far and deep this story traveled.

ACTION STEP: *Describe the best team you were ever on in your life—the most enjoyable, the most efficient. List the components or ingredients that made it so successful. Then consider the role you played in drawing out that success. From there, think of a team you are currently on. What makes it click? What keeps it from succeeding? How could you make things better? This reflection can apply to an athletic team, a work group, a volunteer organization. Pretty much everybody is involved with at least some kind of team. Your spouse and family are your teammates, for that matter. You can link "team" to just about any aspect of your life.*

seven

Stay True to Yourself

You've reached your goals. How do you respond? Has success changed you? Should success change you?

OUR SEASON FOR THE AGES FINALLY ENDED ON Wednesday, March 8, in our state qualifier game against Fairport. The Red Raiders were a terrific team, and even though we'd taken them to overtime earlier in the season and gave them another good run on this night, they led pretty much throughout and we lost 66-58 at Blue Cross Arena. Levar Goff and Rickey Wallace closed out their high school careers in style, scoring twenty-two points each, but our next-highest scorer was Kyle Boline, with four points.

J-Mac was crying. In the closing seconds, when the game was out of reach, he sat on the bench with his head in his hands. After it was over his mother came onto the court to console him. He always took losses very, very hard, and this carried extra emotion because it was the end of the road for him and the other seniors. When you've been riding a wave of success like ours, part of you begins to believe it's never going to end, and it's a shock when that almost inevitably occurs.

We were all disappointed, but overall I think players were extremely satisfied with their accomplishments: a final record of 16-6—including twelve wins in thirteen games after a 4-4 start—along with a league co-championship and sectional crown. I told the guys I was really proud of how far they had come. It seemed that our team upheaval and my near resignation had happened a very long time ago.

A television crew from *Inside Edition* had been following us during the game for a feature that would air nationally the next day. As we headed toward the exit to catch our bus, the players said, "Coach, Jason's not here." I went back into the empty, dark arena, and there was Jason up in the stands with the *Inside Edition* reporter, doing yet another interview. We had to wait another ten minutes for him to finish.

That scene hinted at what lay ahead for both J-Mac and me. The season might have been over, but our lives were now changed by a story that was still growing. Usually I get to enjoy a bit of downtime right after the basketball season ends, but not so in 2005–06. First off, our season had gone long because of our deep playoff run, and I still had tons of letters to read and calls to return. In addition, the list of public appearances was growing long. I was supposed to be the JV tennis coach that spring, but had to hire an assistant because I was going to miss so much time. As for J-Mac, he had to skip outdoor track.

A mere three days after our loss to Fairport, the team was in downtown Rochester as guests for the St. Patrick's Day parade. Cheerleaders and players were in their glory acknowledging the spectators, and J-Mac was the featured attraction as he shot at a basket attached to the back of a float. The setup looked pretty funny, but J-Mac demonstrated that he could adjust to any situation and knocked down most of his shots.

Three mornings after that, on March 14, J-Mac and I took part in another big local event—except this time the whole world was watching, as we met none other than the President of the United States.

As Air Force One touched down at Greater Rochester International Airport, J-Mac, his parents, and I were waiting in a special area to greet President George W. Bush, who was in town for a scheduled appearance in nearby Canandaigua. He had wanted to meet Jason after catching wind of the big game, and then a White House aide called and asked if I'd like to be on hand as well.

I had thought we were going to be in a nice warm room for the meeting, but instead we were right out on the runway, where it was freezing—thirty degrees, with thirty-mile-per-hour winds and some snow to boot. I was both nervous and excited as I watched the president exit the plane. He was all warmth as he gave Jason a hug, got a kiss from the boy's mom, and shook hands with me and Jason's dad. Then the president and Jason interlocked arms and marched up to the national press corps, where Mr. Bush gave a short address:

"First of all, it's great to be here in upstate New York. As you can see, a special person has greeted me at the airport. Uh, Jason, mind if I call you J-Mac? You call me George W." That set off laughter from everyone within earshot.

"Our country was captivated by an amazing story on the basketball court," President Bush continued. "I think it's a story of Coach Johnson's willingness to give a person a chance. It's a story of Dave and Debbie's deep love for their son, and it's a story of a young man who found his touch on the basketball court, which in turn touched the hearts of citizens all across the country."

He turned to Jason and said, "You probably didn't realize the impact you were going to have on people all across America and around the world when you made those six threes in a row." (They didn't actually all come in a row, but I sure wasn't about to correct George W. Bush.) Then he asked me for a placard of Jason's face—we had some extras from the night of February 15—and I gave it to him and he mugged for the cameras with it. The president concluded by saying, "Thank you all for coming, God bless, and I appreciate the wonderful story that's come out of your family."

One of the reporters asked President Bush if he'd seen any of the game footage. He replied that not only had he seen it, but he'd been moved to tears.

His visit with us ended up on national nightly newscasts, and a picture made the front page of the next day's *Washington Post* as well as many other newspapers around the world. No matter what your political persuasion, I think just about all American citizens would consider it a big deal to meet the President. I admired how warm he was to us. He seemed to have a sincere appreciation of our story, and that impressed me, what with all the daily items of importance in his position.

What a turn of events. The previous spring, in 2005, President Bush had come to Greece Athena to give a presentation in our auditorium. Even though the event was held right at the school, only a very limited number of students and staff got to attend, and that did not include either Jason or me. Now here we were, less than a year later, in an exclusive audience with him. Going back to when I had first sought to give Jason some playing time, how could I possibly have fathomed this kind of outcome?

The same day as the presidential visit, I went with a few people from our basketball squad to Spencerport's team banquet. We brought a plaque of appreciation and thanked everyone for being gracious. I'm sure they had encountered some ridicule, because any way you look at it, the deafening cheers on February 15 were due to the fact that somebody was lighting it up against their team. We expressed our respect and admiration for the way they had handled themselves, telling them they were first-class people, and I think they appreciated hearing that. In fact, if you look closely at the video when J-Mac is being engulfed after the game, you can see a Spencerport player clapping in admiration as he walks off the court.

It's also worth remembering that Josh Harter, the Rangers head coach, played a key role in all this. If there hadn't been willingness on his part for Jason to see action on February 15, there would have been no meeting with the president for us. So it was fitting to me that the banquet fell on the same day as President Bush's visit.

On March 19 we had our own team banquet, and of course it was a very special one. Jay Shelofsky, the parent who had produced those blow-up photos of Jason that became such indelible images from the big game, distributed keepsake photograph plaques of our team celebrating the sectional title at mid-court.

On March 26 I did an interview with the BBC; two days later CBS Sports was in town for interviews to air during the NCAA Final Four.

Speaking of the Final Four, we got to be there in person along with the quartet of teams that had qualified: Florida, UCLA, George Mason and LSU. On March 31, Jason, his dad, and I flew to Indianapolis as special guests of General Motors, who sponsored the trip. I had attended three previous Final Fours in my life, but certainly never as an honored guest.

A company representative met us at the airport with two police officers who would be our security, and I thought, "We don't need that." But within a short time, I realized I was walking around with the equivalent of Elvis Presley. Everybody wanted J-Mac's autograph and picture. Later that weekend George McGinnis, who was a fine ABA and NBA player and is popular locally in Indianapolis, found people blowing right by him so they could get to Jason. McGinnis jokingly complained, "J-Mac, I thought *I* was the celebrity here!"

A Coach and a Miracle

We found out we were going to be in the same hotel as Florida's team and that Billy Donovan, the Gators head coach, wanted us to come down to their team dinner. What a thrill for me to chat with Coach Donovan, one of the top coaches in college basketball today and a true class act. Then Jason decided he wanted to meet Glen "Big Baby" Davis, of LSU, and after a couple of phone calls we were on our way to the Tigers' hotel.

General Motors had asked me to give a motivational speech at a dinner that night, and the dealers were excited about hearing the J-Mac story from my perspective and anxious to talk to me when it was over. It was pretty heady stuff for me.

On Saturday, we went by invitation to a George Mason shoot-around a few hours before the Patriots' semifinal game against Florida. George Mason had recently experienced its own miracle, overcoming tremendous odds as a mid-major program to reach the national semifinals. We were given a police escort into the RCA Dome. After practice Jason engaged in an impromptu three-point shooting contest with the Patriots head coach, Jim Larranaga.

> *Never before had a No. 11 seed from a mid-major made a Final Four. Both J-Mac and our George Mason basketball program had the opportunity to live a dream. It's a wonderful thing when people can observe you living your dream. It motivates them to believe that their dreams can come true too.*
>
> — Jim Larranaga

Just prior to the George Mason–Florida game, CBS unveiled its new feature profiling J-Mac. As Jim Nantz introduced the piece, I stood by him on the RCA Dome court in front of a live national television audience along with Jason, his dad, and Mark LaNeve, a vice president with General Motors.

The feature was less about Jason's scoring feat and more about growing up autistic. Right after it ended, Mark LaNeve noted that he is the parent of twin sons affected by autism and encouraged more people to learn about what he described as a very misunderstood disorder. Finally, Jim Nantz put a hand on Jason's shoulder and said with obvious affection, "I want you to know one thing: No matter what happens on this floor this week, my player of the year is right here. Have a great time."

The CBS video would go on to win an Emmy Award for Outstanding Short Feature. Sarah Rinaldi, producer of the segment, said she had an inkling before it was even broadcast of how special it would become. "We showed it in a trailer right before it went on, because people wanted to see the piece. At the end everybody just applauded, wiping their eyes. I've never had a piece that's gotten that kind of feedback," Sarah said, adding that since it had aired, "I've been approached by so many people who are in some way involved in autism organizations or have relatives who are autistic. They absolutely loved the piece, because it was able to demonstrate what kids can do when given the chance."

During the semifinal games we were situated in a terrific luxury box, but that didn't quite work for J-Mac. He wanted to be down by the floor, where the action was. I told him, "Jason, I can't believe it! People would die to be in a luxury box for the Final Four, with all this food and drink."

But for every J-Mac whim that arose, our hosts found an answer. Just like that, two tickets emerged down by the floor for the championship game, so that's where Jason sat on Monday night, with his dad and me splitting time in the other seat. He even got out on the floor to snap some pictures as soon as Florida had completed its 73-57 victory over UCLA. This was arranged through Jim Nantz, who had been quite taken with getting to see Jason face-to-face.

"It was just a tremendous honor to meet him," Jim said. "My favorite memory was having him there for Monday night's championship game. I wanted him to come down when the game ended for the big celebration on the floor—which he was not unfamiliar with—and experience all the atmosphere."

Jason was again flanked by security personnel during the game. My friend Reggie Witherspoon, the University of Buffalo head coach, was sitting in the Florida section and saw the J-Mac phenomenon in action when Jason came through the stands to meet him. As Reggie recalls, the fans' attention shifted right over to Jason, even though their Gators were only minutes away from winning the national championship.

"J-Mac came walking toward me with Jim. He said, 'Coach Willis, I'm J-Mac and I'd like to be your manager next year.' I didn't have the heart to tell him my real name was Witherspoon," Reggie said. "People in our section weren't even paying attention at all to the game, going 'J-Mac, J-Mac, J-Mac,' stopping him to ask for autographs and pictures. We've met many people, from Michael Jordan on down, but J-Mac took on a different level for us, because my wife is a speech therapist and has worked with many autistic people. My wife called our girls at home and told them about it, and they were screaming, 'Oh my God; J-Mac, J-Mac.' My kids thought it was great."

That weekend we met and chatted with such notables as Dick Vitale, Dick Enberg, and Mike Lupica. We even met the grandson of James Naismith, inventor of the game of basketball. I also got to meet John Calipari, who had been so supportive of me in the past by calling me a couple of times even though I was a relatively unknown coach.

After the championship game we were back in the hotel waiting for Florida to return so we could congratulate them. There were many fans waiting in the lobby for the Gators to arrive. J-Mac, his dad, and I were allowed to go up on the balcony above the mass of fans. You would not believe all the cameras flashing, taking pictures of J-Mac. After about thirty minutes, he got very impatient and started wandering around the balcony and down the hall. There were private parties in some of the rooms and J-Mac waltzed right into one of them. His dad was yelling, "Jason, come back here."

We went into the party to retrieve Jason and there he was, talking to none other than Bill Walton. I will never forget his dad yelling Jason's name and then saying in utter shock, "Bill Walton." I almost fell over too—the seven-foot center was the greatest college star from my childhood and had remained very high profile by playing in the NBA and then going into broadcasting. Bill was completely gracious, welcoming us in. We talked to him and his wife for nearly thirty minutes. He reminisced about his days at UCLA under John Wooden and I was enthralled.

Being outside of Rochester gave me a real sense of how this story was affecting the rest of the country. When we got into Indianapolis, we were treated like kings; Jason was the equivalent of a rock star. He seemingly had access to anything he wanted, such as when he chatted up Duke's J. J. Redick and Gonzaga's Adam Morrison after he heard they were in a trailer near us. All season long Jason had joined in debates with his Athena teammates about who was the top player in the country, Redick or Morrison. Now he was rubbing elbows with both of them at the Final Four.

That scene underscored J-Mac's tendency to move toward places he wants to be, even if a sign instructs him otherwise. He had no fear of meeting celebrities that weekend. If they caught his interest, he would sit down and talk to them. If they didn't, he'd simply say hello and keep sauntering right along.

Jason, his parents, and I met one of the biggest celebrities of all on April 12, when we taped an episode of Oprah Winfrey's show in Chicago that was to air a couple of weeks later. Jason was featured as part of a Whiz Kids theme show, and we got to share our story with the biggest daytime-talk-show celebrity of all time. I've always been a great fan of Oprah and her show. I love how she helps people. We were in a room with the other kids and their families before the show. It was fun to meet these extraordinary kids—a piano genius, a national spelling-bee champion, a brother and sister who had performed groundbreaking science research. The one child that I was most impressed with was the fifth-grade boy who planned on running for President of the United States in 2032. He was fascinating to talk to.

The next night we joined the rest of the Greece Athena team in Cleveland for the Cavaliers' NBA game against the New York Knicks. We were all featured on the court for a special ceremony in which the lights were turned off and we were introduced individually. Jason even had some personal time with LeBron James. The game was broadcast by TNT, and Steve Kerr, an ex-NBA guard who was one of their announcers, posed for a photo with his namesake, our tri-captain.

For a couple of days during the Easter break in mid-April, Cheryl Tisa helped me field the many e-mails and letters that had piled up. It was a relief to finally return them, even though it was two months later. I wish I'd done it sooner, because people sent so many beautiful, heartfelt expressions.

New letters kept coming in, as did local and national media requests, as well as invitations to appear at all kinds of events. Stories connected to the night of February 15 were mentioned twenty-one straight days in the *Democrat and Chronicle*. A lot of that had to do not only with J-Mac's accomplishment but also with the availability of game video clips on the Internet.

"In twenty-some-odd years as a reporter, I had never seen a local story blossom into an international story the way this one did," said Scott Pitoniak, who wrote some local columns about us. "I think I'd describe the video as a perfect storm. It really brought the story to life."

Mike Catalana, of WHAM, noted that this was "the biggest local story, by far, that I've ever been involved in. I don't think there's ever been a local story in any way that's had the reach this one did." He agreed that J-Mac's feat would never have resonated so strongly "if it wasn't for the video of him actually doing it. The fact that it wasn't network-quality video, to me, made it even better. It gave you the feeling that you were looking in on something never meant for television. Actually having the team video that was so electric made it work so much better."

National media, as well, contended that there were intangibles in the video that went beyond J-Mac and his baskets.

"The best thing about this besides Jason's feeling of euphoria was to see the reaction of the student body," said my friend Jeff Van Gundy. "It just warms my heart. You hear about kids excluding each other and all the bad things, but that night you saw where the kids in the stands and the players celebrated their differences. You don't see teenagers express true joy in a lot of things in their life, and that was a moment of true joy."

"Seeing the students rush out of the bleachers and put Jason on their shoulders, I'm actually getting a little teary-eyed just thinking about it again," added Seth Davis, of CBS and *Sports Illustrated*. "It gives you chills. The real story was the reaction of the students; I think they were happier for Jason than he was for himself. The story encompassed the entire team and student body, and not just one kid."

It was truly a Hollywood ending, and thus there had been plenty of interest from major Hollywood studios about making a movie of Jason's life, in which my character would be featured as well. Columbia Pictures won the derby, and Earvin "Magic" Johnson had emerged as an executive producer. As part of that agreement, the Basketball Hall of Famer paid a visit to Greece Athena on April 26.

What an outing. Magic gave an assembly for the entire student body in our auditorium and cracked lots of jokes while flashing that million-dollar smile. He also emphasized the importance of education, then posed for all kinds of pictures in the gym with Jason, me, the team, and the cheerleaders. Jason gave a quick speech of his own that day.

The next month J-Mac went to a banquet in Syracuse, where he was presented with an award by Gerry McNamara, star guard for Syracuse University. It was the first meeting ever between J-Mac and G-Mac, who had served as my inspiration for the nickname I had bestowed upon Jason two years earlier. Just a couple of weeks after J-Mac's big game, G-Mac had staged a rather miraculous performance of his own to close out his collegiate career: He hit several last-second shots as the Orange won four games in as many days to capture the Big East tournament.

"I think Gerry must have gotten the inspiration for that from J-Mac. Both events were almost surreal in that they happened back-to-back like that. Both guys seemed to be touched by something quite incredible," said Syracuse coach Jim Boeheim, one of the most successful college coaches in history and a Basketball Hall of Famer.

Three years earlier, McNamara had scored six three-point baskets to spark the Orange to their national championship win over Kansas. And guess what? Six three-pointers is exactly how many J-Mac amassed on the night of February 15.

"It's quite curious. No question there are more similarities than just their nicknames," Coach Boeheim added. He further observed that both J-Mac and G-Mac are smaller-than-average guards who still found ways to come up big and make national splashes, thanks to their work ethic and determination.

Jay Wright, a Big East cohort of Jim Boeheim's who has been a friend of mine since he coached at the University of Rochester, agreed with the comparison. "You always have a couple of guys like that—little, scrappy guys that kind of make their shortcomings, if you will, their greatest strength. G-Mac and J-Mac—you have to love them and respect them, be inspired by them every day," Jay remarked.

Our team went up to Albany on June 6 to meet Governor George Pataki and several other political dignitaries. The trip was arranged by Joseph Robach, our state senator from Greece. Governor Pataki greeted us all and posed for some pictures, then said, "Well, you know, I used to play some basketball. Coach, grab a couple of players."

He had a basket set up outside the Governor's Mansion, and next thing I knew, the governor had peeled off his suit coat and was scrimmaging with J-Mac and other guys on the team. "J-Mac is probably still bragging about how he smoked me from the corner," he was to later quip. The game came to an abrupt end when Brian Benson, my center, decided to show off with a slam dunk and broke the rim.

"We've had all kinds of people at the state capitol—Syracuse's national champions, presidents, foreign dignitaries. But my colleagues were very excited about meeting Jason. No matter who you were, it was a story that in one way or another could hit home about somebody doing the right thing, sticking to it, and having it pay off," Senator Robach said. "Once that story got on national TV and even became a part of national conversation, and knowing it was from your town, I'd say that's absolutely wonderful. It's one of the best stories ever of human accomplishment. It happened right in Greece and people will be talking about it for a long time to come."

The events rolled on and on through the spring. We were special guests at the Rochester Press-Radio Club dinner, sharing the dais with football great Peyton Manning. A declaration of Jason's accomplishment was made in Congress. The team got to meet Hillary Clinton, then a New York state senator, at a state teachers' meeting. Jason threw out the opening pitch at a Rochester Red Wings baseball game and the team also had a Bobblehead

Night with a figure in his likeness. J-Mac became team manager for the Rochester RazorSharks, our local pro basketball team. There was a rap song made about him. There was a Jason McElwain Day held by the Town of Greece, as well as a J-Mac Night at our local McDonald's, with Jason and his teammates playing the role of waiters.

Features eventually appeared in *People, Reader's Digest,* and *Sports Illustrated* magazines. We got mentioned by Dave Anderson in the *New York Times,* Mike Lupica in the *Daily News,* and Bob Verdi in the *Chicago Tribune.* I got to write an article through my own eyes for *Guideposts* magazine. One side of me wanted things to slow down, to get my life back. But most of the ride was an absolute blast.

This included one rather odd occurrence. I was supposed to receive a National Sportsmanship Award on June 10 in St. Louis, but organizers got Greece Athena mixed up with Spencerport High School. So the invitation accidentally went to Spencerport, leading the Rangers basketball coach, Josh Harter, to believe the sportsmanship honor was meant for him.

When the banquet officials clarified that they wanted the coach of J-Mac, Josh was disappointed. I stated that I could not accept the award without Josh being included, since he played a significant part in the recognition I was receiving. To their credit, the organizers reworked things so that we could be co-recipients, and we both went to St. Louis. A highlight of the banquet was meeting broadcaster Bob Costas, who congratulated both of us for our actions on the night of February 15.

ABC/ESPN produced a follow-up feature on Jason, which aired June 15 on ABC during Game 4 of the NBA Finals and later appeared on the ESPY Awards show. Once again the autism angle was probed in-depth, as interviewer Tom Rinaldi profiled two parents who had written to Jason thanking him for providing hope for the future of their young autistic son.

Then came the ESPY Awards on July 12. Jason's big night had been nominated for Best Moment, and he was up against three very worthy nominees: Kobe Bryant's eighty-one-point game; George Mason's run to the NCAA Final Four; and teen golfer Dakoda Dowd playing a pro event in front of her terminally ill mother.

That's mighty stiff competition. Kobe's eighty-one points, set January 22 with the Los Angeles Lakers against the Toronto Raptors, is the second-highest total in NBA history. George Mason was one of the great underdog stories of all time, and the Dowd family's story just tugs at your heartstrings.

When Jason was announced as the winner, he got a standing ovation from the ESPY audience, which included Kobe himself—the very guy Jason used to idolize, even calling himself Kobe McElwain.

Jason read his acceptance speech from his notes, and as he thanked his family, friends, and teammates, his voice started to shake, which rarely happened when he spoke publicly. "Most importantly of all, I would like to thank my loving coach that helped us get a Section 5 championship, Coach Johnson, for giving me the chance to play," he said. I was really touched that Jason would single me out. He closed the speech by saying emphatically, "Thank you, God."

On August 12, J-Mac and I traveled to Texas for a function benefiting the charitable organization of the San Antonio Spurs' Robert Horry, and Robert graciously took us out to lunch.

A week later, our whole team was flown out to Los Angeles for the Fox Teen Choice Awards, where J-Mac was given the Courage Award. I had been contacted by the organizers, who said they wanted to surprise Jason by bringing his whole team out on stage. We were put up in a separate hotel and showed up unannounced when he got his award. It was a great scene: The players were in full uniform, and I joined them in storming out on stage chanting "J-Mac" as the crowd shrieked. We all started jumping up and down with J-Mac and hugging him before the players once more put him on their shoulders. He then read a speech similar to the one he gave at the ESPYs and capped it off by screaming, "God bless America!"

What a treat that trip was for the kids. They were given passes to all kinds of theme parks, restaurants, and shops. They got to meet all the big stars for their age group—Ashley Olsen, Brooke Hogan, Snoop Dogg, Wilmer Valderrama, Rihanna, Dane Cook, Jessica Simpson. Being on the team that year was something the players would never forget, given all the special events they got to attend. I guess you could consider it a reward for all we had been through earlier in the season.

I talked to Ashton Kutcher for a couple of minutes at the Fox event. I'll never forget him saying he had wanted to meet me because he thought I did something very special. And I'm thinking, "Wow, *he* wants to meet *me*?" It's fascinating to me how people in very high places responded to this story. I guess what I've learned is that whether it's fellow coaches, the President, people on the street, rich people, or poor people, we can all be inspired equally by a single event.

We got another surge of publicity in many TV and newspaper end-of-the-year reviews of the biggest stories of 2006, as our saga's staying power endured. But I'm not going to lie and say everybody was enthralled by every aspect of the J-Mac phenomenon. First of all, lots of people in the general public were puzzled as to why I hadn't played J-Mac earlier in the season. The outspoken Charles Barkley even kidded on the air, as only Charles Barkley can, that I should have been fired for not playing J-Mac more. My supportive colleagues taped that quote over my desk at school.

When faced with that question on the media rounds, I just jokingly said that J-Mac was our secret weapon. But in my heart and mind I knew he was a one-dimensional player, and that reality gets obscured in the video clip of his scoring outburst. Jason made no defensive play of note on February 15, didn't pass, didn't have a rebound, and dribbled only once or twice.

Other critics felt that J-Mac had it too easy, that Spencerport let up on him. It is true that sometimes a kid with a severe disability is set up so he can score a basket or a touchdown, but I don't feel that happened with Spencerport. True, they weren't trying to block his shots, but they did play some amount of defense. In fact, as I've already mentioned, the one time they did give him an uncontested layup, he missed it! Let's also remember how hard it is to hit three-pointers consistently. If you make six out of ten practicing by yourself, that's awfully good. There's nothing easy about making a basket from almost twenty feet away and beyond.

Among the hundreds of positive letters I received, there was a negative one declaring that our team should have been assessed a technical foul on February 15 because the crowd rushed the floor a couple of seconds before the game ended. Yes, a rule had been skirted, but I believe that the officials, Mike Padulo and Lloyd Collins, had needed to make a commonsense decision in that situation. Besides, we won by thirty-eight points, so certainly the game's outcome wasn't affected by not calling a technical.

But the overwhelming majority of correspondence focused only on the good that came out of J-Mac's performance. By this point Jason had become a genuine pop idol, and the attention was pretty daunting for the entire McElwain family. David and Debbie saw their son thrust into a celebrity role without warning, after having been a fairly anonymous team manager. They didn't want him exploited, because sharks inevitably circle when somebody becomes this famous, and Jason's age and disability made it tougher to fend those sharks off.

Around school and the town of Greece, Jason couldn't go anywhere without getting stopped for an autograph, handshake, or photo. He took a date to the senior ball and others were asking him to the prom. He was definitely a hot commodity.

"For the rest of the year it was amazing how differently the kids treated him—'Hey, there he is, there he is,'" Andy McCormack said. "Somebody wanted to go to the prom with him who hadn't been that friendly to him before. People in his classroom finally became sick of all the fuss."

Jason and I continued to hit the banquet and interview circuit, often together. During this time our bond got even stronger. He was confident that I would help him with any type of interview, and I would encourage him, telling him he did a great job.

Jason generally took the attention in stride. His personality really seemed to work in his favor. It was neat to see him continue to grow and gain confidence. Early on in interviews he had been somewhat overwhelmed, and that really changed. Jason got very comfortable in front of a camera. Through it all, his sweetness prevailed. He never lost that sense of humbleness; once he had become a national media darling he still maintained his team-first attitude. He developed a little ritual of ending his interviews by giving special hellos to certain people—teammates, friends in his neighborhood.

The whirlwind of activity was surreal. My view on fame has evolved into "Wow, if you had to do this every day it would be a real challenge." I now understand why celebrities need other people taking their calls and attending to their affairs. I also can see how they might get unfairly judged simply because they want to be left alone.

That being stated, I also became acutely aware of my obligation to give back to my community, to honor God by spreading inspirational messages. People were going to connect me with J-Mac for years to come, and I had to be a good steward of the story. Meanwhile, Jason had become a shining light for the autistic community in terms of raising public awareness about the disability. In fact, many of our appearances have been for youth and special-needs organizations, such as when we attended the dedication of a new group home in Greece.

I began acquiring speaking engagements both locally and out of town, and I quickly developed a theme of "dreams really do come true." For a long time I had wanted to get into motivational speaking anyway, and now I had a great story to tell and people who wanted to hear it.

It was imperative to me that, having acquired somewhat of a celebrity status, I remained true to my core values—how I want to treat people; how I want to be treated. For example, I made sure I answered every piece of congratulatory correspondence that came my way, even though it took months. I was not about to let the distractions change me as a person. It always comes back to a simple philosophy of allowing God to guide me toward doing the right thing.

If there was one fear I had, it was that I'd be expected to know a lot about autism and other disabilities. Certainly I've learned much about autism through being with J-Mac, but an expert I am not. I said as much to organizers when I was invited to speak at a school for autism in Delaware, but the neat thing is how they reacted: "That's not what we're looking for, Coach. We just want you to share your story and give us hope." I did go there to speak, and it went great.

ACTION STEP: *Think of the people who have helped you over the years, particularly those you no longer see regularly. Show a sign of appreciation by sending a note, making a phone call, firing off an e-mail, paying a visit. As you've moved into a better place in life— fame, athletic achievements, professional success, whatever—do you remember those who went out of their way to assist you in getting there? Do you carry on those same qualities of helpfulness to the people around you? Have you remained polite, respectful, and thoughtful to* *all kinds of folks? Are you diligent about returning correspondence as soon as possible?*

eight

Share Your Success

Will your accomplishments help make the world a better place?
God wants your actions to not only improve your life, but to
inspire success in others too.

WHEN MIKE CATALANA, SPORTS DIRECTOR OF
WHAM, in Rochester, called me two nights after J-Mac's twenty-point game asking for my approval to send his news report out
nationally, I thought, "That would be great, because it would give
hope to a lot of people."

Still, I couldn't have imagined just how many folks would
be impacted until feedback started pouring in—hundreds and
hundreds of expressions of congratulations for J-Mac and me.

I've held on to all my letters and e-mails. There are so many
interesting and touching stories in that vault, especially those
shared by parents, educators, and organizations—even some
autistic people—who deal daily with such disabilities as autism
spectrum disorders, attention deficit disorder, mental retardation, and developmental disabilities. College students wrote
in, noting that their interest in studying special education was
heightened by this story. Their correspondence conveyed earnest-
ness, excitement, and emotion. I'd say close to half of the letter

writers acknowledged that the story moved them to tears. Others simply stated that this feel-good sports saga was a refreshing contrast to news of superstar athletes carping over multimillion-dollar contracts.

It was awesome to hear from a number of Division I head coaches, some of whom are personal friends, and others who simply wanted to express their support of my decision to allow Jason to play basketball on February 15. One of my most cherished letters came from Billy Donovan, head coach at the University of Florida, whom Jason and I met along with his team at the Final Four just before the Gators won the 2006 national championship. What Billy described about his own title squad could well have applied to my young men at Greece Athena in 2005–06.

"To have the opportunity to work with such an unselfish group of players and staff is rewarding beyond words," Billy wrote. "They represent all that can be accomplished through hard work and love and care for one another. This was a tremendous experience because of how everybody involved was totally selfless and concerned about the next person."

Other celebrities who got in touch included ESPN's Dick Vitale, who sent a nice handwritten letter expressing his hope to meet Jason and me (which did eventually occur at the Final Four); David J. Barrett, creator of "One Shining Moment," the song played at the conclusion of each year's NCAA tournament broadcast on CBS, who commented, "When I heard this story, my first thought was, 'This is why I wrote this song'"; and Tom Donahoe, former executive for the NFL's Pittsburgh Steelers and Buffalo Bills, who told me, "Having been involved with sports for thirty-eight years I have seen a lot of incredible things happen. Nothing will ever come close to the Jason McElwain story. What you did for that young man is something you will never top if you coach for thirty more years." A Nike employee even wrote to let me know that Mark Parker, the company's CEO, had paid homage to the J-Mac event in a company-wide newsletter.

Whereas these types of letters were quite touching, others were cause for a good chuckle. A high school basketball manager from North Carolina pitched the idea of him playing Jason one-on-one on ESPN at Greece Athena, provided we pick up his travel expenses; one woman wanted to know if J-Mac's twenty-point game really happened or was just an urban legend (and who could blame her for doubting the authenticity of such a feat?); and somebody else wanted to know just where Greece, New York, is. I was also amused at how J-Mac's name was massacred in print, even from folks who otherwise appeared to be good spellers: McElwaine, McElwin, Mr. James McAlvin, Jason Mckelway, McElroy, T-Mac, McElwayne. One note referred to him as J-Lo, as in Jennifer Lopez. I didn't feel so bad anymore about having been unable to pronounce J-Mac's last name when I first knew him.

Lots of letters were sent by personal acquaintances—family members, fellow school district employees, current and old friends, former players and students. A onetime teammate from my Greece Arcadia playing days got in touch and noted that he has a son with Asperger's syndrome, an autism spectrum disorder. A longtime Section 5 basketball official remarked that if anybody followed this story on video and didn't tear up, "they probably have created medical history for living without a heart or soul."

Frank Vito, a veteran educator in the Greece Central School District who has also been heavily involved in Special Olympics, agreed with my contention that a seemingly simple gesture had morphed into a bona fide miracle. In fact, several letter writers compared Jason's feat to the 1980 Miracle on Ice, when the United States Olympic hockey team won the gold medal in Lake Placid, New York. Many others mentioned Wilt Chamberlain's hundred-point game in 1962, which still stands as an NBA single-game record. Imagine if J-Mac had scored twenty points in the *first* four minutes of the game and continued to play. He was well above a hundred-point pace for the time that he played.

Our basketball team's early-season struggles had coincided with a tension-filled year in the Greece district due to administrative upheaval. Many teachers from the district sent me notes of thanks, simply because our overwhelmingly positive story gave them a morale boost and helped put Greece back in its rightful place as a school system to be respected. Other letters alluded to our basketball team's behind-the-scenes strife in 2005–06, but that type of correspondence was minimal because our troubles had largely stayed out of the public eye.

Most letters came from people I'd never met and never will meet. The J-Mac phenomenon, I discovered, had become the inspiration for essays, poems, songs, and sermons. Correspondence rained down from nearly all fifty states, not to mention many foreign countries. Some folks, including two young men who had once been foreign exchange students at Greece Athena, noted that they had seen news coverage on German television. In fact, one of them, Michael Scheyer, served as a student basketball assistant for me in the mid-1990s—essentially an earlier version of J-Mac.

Several notes came from England. One London resident stated that he was "gobsmacked" by the event. (Don't you love that word?) He added that he wanted to congratulate all of us even though we had "probably received a thousand letters saying the same thing." Well, I can assure this gentleman that no other letter writer mentioned having been gobsmacked.

Australia was another place where this story apparently hit big, based on the feedback I got. I heard from the mother of a learning-disabled child. I also heard from a mom of an autistic son; she was compiling a book of stories from the parents of autistic kids worldwide. Elsewhere on the other side of the world, one letter writer noted that he had seen the J-Mac highlights via CBS on the BBC in Israel. A request came from Spain for Jason to be the guest of honor at a high school basketball tournament. The coach of a professional team in Germany proposed having J-Mac sign a contract for two weeks, guaranteeing that he would play in at least one game.

Speaking of coaches, quite a few letters alluded in some form to the roles and responsibilities of coaching. Several of my brethren shared their appreciation for my actions in J-Mac's success story, while also noting that they had performed similar gestures by including special-needs children on their teams. Many parents also wrote to express their admiration for coaches who had accommodated their children's special situations.

One youth coach told how he'd made room on his roster for a boy who had spent his life in a wheelchair. Though the boy never played, his teams won state championships in baseball and football and he served as an obvious inspiration to his teammates, the coach stated.

A football coach recalled that his special-needs godson served as a team assistant, "and nothing made my godson smile more than retrieving footballs before our games, when my son was kicking extra points. We always used to congratulate him when we made the extra points [during the games] and would tell him it was his help that made it happen. He would always respond that he was having a good day and would get very excited."

One father wrote that his son has cerebral palsy and uses a motorized chair, but still served as manager of his high school basketball team: "His mentor and the coach of the team took my son into his program four years ago and changed his life. Very few people know or even realize what a difference this made in the life of my son, and to the people in the basketball program."

One mother told of her autistic son's similar success story: "Our family was very fortunate to have our son attend a high school that embraced him and he too had a high school basketball coach that took him under his wing and helped him develop. While [he] never played on the team or got a chance to get in the game, he did score a basket during PE class that brought the house down!"

A developmentally disabled girl belonged to her high school cheerleading squad, albeit in a limited role. "But it really does not matter to her or us that much," her mother wrote. "[She] is happy as a clam; you can't wipe the smile off her face when she has that uniform on! She has tremendous school spirit, and absolutely LOVES being a part of the squad. She's made new friends, and I think the other girls and coaches and parents are getting to know [her] better, for who she is and not what her disability is."

A young man who had been captain of his high school football team recounted how an autistic boy was allowed to play in one of his team's games: "Although he didn't have quite the success J-Mac had, I saw the excitement in his eyes when he was put into the game and I know it was very special for him."

One dad observed the long-term effects of inclusion for his son with Asperger's syndrome: "[He] volunteered as manager for his varsity football team and with much concern my wife and I allowed him. His varsity coach, the assistant coaches, teammates, and school students all supported [him] throughout the year and he has blossomed because he was included." The father noted that his son had gone on to college and was "doing wonderfully well. My wife and I firmly believe his experience with his classmates and teammates has made a significant contribution to his growth and will lead him successfully into the future."

A special-education teacher told me that he recorded the news clip about J-Mac and played it at a meeting: "Our team of special ed teachers couldn't wait for me to hit 'play' because I've been raving about the story! There wasn't a dry eye in the room. We, as educators, know that giving students 'a shot' truly inspires our mission to help students succeed and feel proud of their accomplishments. I guess that's why we do what we do."

All of these letters follow a vital theme, which is the high value of practicing inclusiveness. They also helped remind me that although I'm the one who garnered considerable media attention because of the twenty points J-Mac scored, in truth I was representing lots of other coaches who strive to create similar opportunities. For that reason, I've felt rather funny about having received so many individual accolades. Whatever kudos have come my way, I accept them on behalf of the many coaches out there who would have done exactly the same thing with J-Mac had they been in my shoes.

Unfortunately, some parents expressed anguish to me as well. They noted that their kids would have liked nothing more than to get the same chance as J-Mac, but that moment never came. A mom recounted how her son with Down syndrome wanted to play basketball in high school and junior high: "He has wanted to be on the bowling team, golf team, soccer team, football team, swimming team, and basketball team. We have talked to coaches, principals, and the superintendent, and all in vain. [He] graduates in May and will never be given the opportunity that you gave to Jason. We know he can do it, [he] knows he can do it, but no one gave him an opportunity."

This feeling of frustration can also apply to kids who make the team but remain glued to the bench, observed a father of three who acknowledged that his kids were not great athletes: "I am sure that there are many kids out there who don't get that chance to be great or even compete—just because they are different. They are taught the lessons, but continue to ride the pine at the end of the bench or pick up the towels, without ever getting to wear the uniform. The 'team concept' applies to everyone, except for the different kid."

A couple of coaches told me they rued the fact that they had never put their team manager, special-needs or otherwise, into a game at some point. Then again—and I walk a bit on eggshells on this next point—it's not all that simple for a coach, who has a number of responsibilities, to accommodate a student with obvious athletic limitations. In fact, the coach might have perfectly legitimate reasons for not throwing the door open to any and every kid who wants to join in.

Actually, we *do* throw the door open, insofar as any student with proper medical clearance is allowed to participate in tryouts. Then when I make cuts, it's strictly based on who are the best players. It doesn't matter if they're autistic or not, or whether they're black, white, Asian, or Hispanic. Cutting is always a painful process for me, but it does come down to that basic reality of who the best players are. I'm not out to get anyone, but I do end up saying no much more than yes. I might have twice as many guys try out as my roster will allow, and even after cuts are made I can still play only five people at a time.

So it helps if people can have a sense of balance, if those inspired by J-Mac's success don't think their child is going to go out and score twenty points in the next game. Consider the perspective of one letter writer describing the high school sports involvement of her son with Asperger's syndrome:

"He tries really hard, but as you well know with autistic kids it doesn't always happen. The coaches here try hard, but it is hard when you are behind in the score to put someone in who doesn't have the capabilities of other kids. For instance, [he] gets confused out on the lacrosse field sometimes on where he is supposed to be and that costs him playing time," she wrote, also acknowledging that her son's social limitations don't help the situation. "The other hard thing is that Asperger's is high-functioning autism and to most people [he] looks normal, except his social skills are really bad and this turns people off and they don't want to listen to him or deal with him." She stated that she cried at the newscast about J-Mac, "because it was so great to see a child like mine actually making it."

Despite the outcome on February 15, it wasn't a snap decision for me to say Jason should play or even that he should be team manager. If for whatever reason a manager cannot perform his job well, that can have a negative effect on everybody. The coach still has a team to run and cannot afford an inordinate amount of distractions.

Early in a child's life, with the availability of beginner sports leagues that emphasize participation, it's much more likely that a special-needs athlete will get the chance to play. There are also wonderful opportunities through Special Olympics. However, I am a varsity coach, and at that level, with crowded gyms and a bigger emphasis on winning and losing, I have to weigh each situation very carefully before putting somebody with question-able skills into a contest. The last thing a coach wants to do is open up the door for humiliation, ridicule, and resentment.

So, what some may perceive as an uncaring attitude may actu-ally be a coach's desire to protect the well-being of a special-needs student. That's part of why I held Jason out of the Spencerport game until we had it well in hand. Even then, I was a nervous wreck up until he made his first basket, because he had missed his first shot by a mile and then blown a layup.

I'd be sending the wrong message if I didn't reiterate these points. But let me also make clear that I strongly empathize with all the parents out there who love their kids to pieces and who go to any length necessary to help them succeed. Therefore I chal-lenge all coaches of young people to keep their eyes and ears open for situations that might benefit at least one special-needs student. Any coach of youth sports needs to be extra-conscious of being a good role model whenever possible. Assigning respon-sibility to somebody who isn't blessed with physical ability but wants to be a part of something is a great way to teach life lessons about acceptance and inclusion. If you can't make that happen by giving such a person a roster spot, then a manager's or assistant's position could be a very natural fit—even a role as simple as getting water and towels for the players during games.

Of course, sports is by no means the only the area of school life in which inclusion can be practiced. Based on the letters I got from school districts around the country, efforts toward main-streaming special-needs students are occurring more and more. For example, a teacher from the Baltimore area noted that "we have several students with the same disability as Jason and I'm sure you know what great kids they are. We involve our kids in extracurricular activities and it makes them shine."

It's vital for special-needs students to be accepted not only by the coach but also by the players, not only by the administrators and teachers but also by the students. That's another area in which I'm proud to say Greece Athena scores very high marks, since media reports correctly portrayed Jason as a valued and beloved member of our squad by his teammates. That was never more evident than when my players made sure Jason got so many scoring opportunities on February 15.

"We have a son who is 7 and has autism," one set of parents wrote. "We can't tell you how thrilled we are to know that people like you exist in the world and are willing to give these children a chance. Please, could you also thank those players who PASSED THE BALL TO JASON, as they are also worthy of our thanks."

Along with the players, what kind of role could the rest of the student body play? Is there a chance that an autistic person could be included in the student cheering section? To what degree can teens move past the cliques and jock mentality and have some genuine compassion for the special-needs population? How can we all go about fostering a sense of belonging so that special-needs students can have good memories to take from their scholastic experience?

To this end, letter writers expressed a universal admiration for how our Athena student body embraced Jason on February 15, both before and after his scoring eruption.

"Autism is a neurological disorder that can cause the individual to feel isolated and very lonely . . . [but] I never have seen such love come from young adults," a grandmother of an autistic child wrote.

"It is clear that Jason and his differences from most of the student body are not simply tolerated," added an Athena graduate whose son has autism. "Autistic children need most to feel safe and comfortable in their environment, to function at their best. You and your staff as well as the students have given Jason that comfort and safety. This is a culture of inclusion that is plain to see in the video of that night and all of the interviews that followed."

A father of four-year-old autistic twins wrote that he's "always wondering how far they will go in life and what we will all have to endure. You and your whole school should be commended for how Jason is treated, loved, and respected. Kids can be harsh, and to see how Jason was put on all their shoulders put a tear in my eye."

On the other hand, another writer ventured—accurately—that support for Jason had not always been as universal as it seemed in the video: "Perhaps there were some whose acts towards Jason prior to Feb. 15, 2006, were not so noble as most, that were downright mean or cruel. If they were present in that gym, or saw the reports, I'm hopeful they realized the error of their ways."

Special-needs people indeed can be easy targets, because not only do they stand out from the crowd but they also find it difficult to fight back. "Kids can be very cruel," remarked one mother whose autistic son struggled to fit in while in high school. Added the mother of a fourteen-year-old with attention deficit hyperactivity disorder (ADHD), "I cannot tell you how many times I have cried leaving the hockey rink and the lacrosse field after games and practice as the boys shove him aside and cast him off because he is not as good as they are."

True, J-Mac's heroics aren't going to erase all the difficult aspects of living with a disability, either for him or for others with similar diagnoses. As one school social worker put it, special-needs students seemingly face more challenges daily than other people do in a lifetime.

But it's for that very reason—that the road is long and difficult—that correspondents also poured out unmitigated joy. J-Mac had burst through his own roadblocks and had opened the door for thousands of people like him. Letter writers were happy for Jason, happy for me, happy for our school, and more upbeat about their own kids' futures.

Not surprisingly, this sentiment was most frequently expressed by families of autistic children. Even though there is no known cause of autism or cure for the disability, parent after parent emphasized how this story gave them hope.

A father of a four-year-old boy with autism acknowledged that "one of the biggest fears is that my son will be alienated from and will never be given the same opportunity as his peers. I just wanted to thank you for quelling those fears." Another dad noted that it was his daughter's fifth birthday on the day he wrote to me. "She is a sweet, lovable kid with autism, he wrote. "Birthdays are a mixed blessing and I was having a few down minutes when I saw the story on TV of J-Mac. You and your student body did a nice thing and it truly touched me. I'm always looking for inspiration and you helped me today. Thank you!"

Earlier I mentioned that many college coaches got in touch with me. Interestingly, three of them have an autistic child, including Steve Donahue, then the head coach of Cornell University. "I just finished watching the video on Jason. It brought tears to my eyes," Donahue wrote. "As a father of an autistic child I can't thank you enough for what you did for Jason—but more importantly what you did for the players, parents, and fans of your basketball team. By accepting Jason into your program you educated them about all the special qualities that autistic children have and what joy they can bring us all."

This letter from a highly respected coach serves as a reminder that autism touches all kinds of families, whether you're a doctor, lawyer, coach, or blue-collar worker. Soledad O'Brien, of CNN, mentioned to Jason and me during a live interview that she has a nephew with autism. Mark LaNeve, a high-ranking official with General Motors, told a national television audience during the Final Four about his two autistic children. Every time word can get out to the masses like this, it advances efforts for medical research into the disorder and helps erase mistaken social assumptions that autistic people are retarded or just plain weird.

Without his knowing it at the time, the baskets Jason scored on February 15 made him a poster boy for autism, an invaluable source for raising awareness. One letter writer mentioned that he was going to forward the game video to all of his friends with autistic children, which may not seem like a particularly significant gesture until you consider how many other people may have done the same thing.

A father of a six-year-old boy with autism, who is on the board of directors for his state's autism society, noted that he "pushed this message out to as many people as I could and beyond because of what this brilliant young lad had accomplished." And yet another dad of a six-year-old autistic boy wrote, "What you have done to raise awareness of autism worldwide would have taken years by conventional means."

One mother of a twelve-year-old autistic boy observed that perhaps this miracle involving J-Mac will point out what children like hers bring to the table, rather than what they lack: "I actually think it's a blessing in disguise for those of us as parents to be blessed with such gifted children." As you can tell, I learned a lot of poignant details about people's lives through their letters. They related stories not just about their children, but about other challenges they're experiencing, at work, home, or elsewhere. One example is the father of four youngsters, who stated, "I am not with any group or organization. I am just a young man that tries to use whatever means to raise my children right. Jason's story is one that every child should be taught."

So many folks expressed the need for a feel-good story and how the miracle night at Greece Athena lifted them up. It's sobering to hear both from people affected by disabilities and from the large number who suffer all other kinds of heartache and hardship. You have to feel for this veteran police officer from the inner city of Oakland and Stockton, California: "I have seen some of the worst things humankind has to offer. I work hard to remain optimistic about the state of the world, to believe it's still a decent place. Your actions help me to affirm my beliefs. I know your family, faculty, students, and community are very proud of you. I don't even know you and I'm proud of you. Thanks and God bless you."

An army veteran noted that he served in Iraq and survived nightly attacks by insurgents. He called J-Mac's performance "the most prolific sports moment of the decade" and stated that the miracle has "inspired a country, a state, a city, and a school, not to mention a war vet typing through tears."

A nurse described seeing "a lot of really bad things and sick people every day, and unfortunately, some of that comes home with me every night. The Lord rewarded me by letting me stumble across a video clip that would brighten my spirits for a long, long time."

A police officer, a soldier, a nurse. I also got a nice letter from a firefighter. The common link here is dedication to service. It is highly admirable work, but folks in these positions are also high burnout candidates and could stand some inspiration from time to time.

Other people who cited challenging situations include a man who lost his son in 2002 to cerebral palsy; a dad all the way from Austria who was going to show the game video to his wife because she had been "very down" about their one-year-old daughter with epilepsy; and a mother of three whose longtime husband had recently left the family for a younger woman, and who wanted Jason to sign a provided basketball for her son as a high school graduation present. The ball was indeed signed and returned.

One Greece Athena graduate wrote from New Orleans, where her home had recently been rebuilt after Hurricane Katrina. Commenting on the J-Mac story, she wrote, "It was fabulous to witness a positive note in the news (we are inundated with the local depressing scene of New Orleans' slow and painful rebuilding process six months post-Katrina), and to know it was my hometown, and my alma mater, that was proudly supporting the endeavor was fabulous. Keep up the good work—go Trojans!"

It's clear that J-Mac's miracle night signified a lot more than some basketball game being played in upstate New York. I've mentioned at length how the night of February 15 marked the culmination of my passion, mission, goals, and perseverance, and Jason's as well. It's so awesome to know how this achievement mattered deeply not just to the two of us, but to people worldwide.

Obviously the J-Mac story strikes a special chord with people who can relate to living with disabilities. But I think this tale accessed something way down inside everyone, something deeply human and deeply spiritual. This was a victory for the underdog, and we could all join in the celebration—which is exactly how I believe God wanted the script to go.

I still get letters every so often. Keep them coming! Thanks to everyone for writing in. You've hit me with a whole mailbag full of life lessons.

ACTION STEP: *Give back. Donate money to worthy causes, but don't stop at that. Consider how you might donate your time and talent via volunteerism and advocacy, stumping for people who in some respects aren't as fortunate as you. For me, especially since the J-Mac experience, it's unthinkable not to be involved in causes related to education, coaching, and the special-needs population. Another dimension of sharing success is acknowledging others in their moments of triumph, not always demanding that the spotlight remain on you. I still send lots of handwritten notes of congratulations. As I've grown as a person, I really get a kick out of doing that. It makes* me *feel good.*

nine

Believe in Miracles

Do you believe that God can perform miracles? Do you have the faith and hope that you can be witness to a miracle that will positively affect your life?

The greatest discovery of my generation is that human beings can alter their lives by altering their attitudes of mind.

—William James

The secret of life isn't what happens to you, but what you do with what happens to you.

—Norman Vincent Peale

Nothing great has ever been accomplished without enthusiasm.

—Ralph Waldo Emerson

Real integrity is doing the right thing knowing that nobody's going to know whether you did it or not.

—Oprah Winfrey

THESE ARE ALL "QUOTES OF THE WEEK" THAT I shared with my team during the 2005–06 season. Who knows how much impact any single quote had, and on which individuals? That's not something you can measure, but I do know that was a year I didn't feel my breath was wasted.

A Coach and a Miracle

To me, the miracle of February 15, 2006, was a culmination of all the life lessons I had imparted on my team—the weekly quotes, the emphasis on doing the right thing. I had a real feeling of validation that I'd been doing things basically right. "Great is your reward in heaven," I've heard at Sunday Mass all my life. The way I understand that Bible quotation, you do the right thing without wondering what you stand to gain or how somebody might pay you back during your lifetime. You don't keep a scorecard.

As coaches, we're gratified when former players have gone on to star in college or perhaps even enter the coaching ranks. Many have built successful careers totally removed from athletics. Every once in a while we might receive a thank-you note expressing how we played a formative role in that person's life. Still, the exact level of impact you have on most kids' lives will never be known. I consider myself among the fortunate ones because through the J-Mac experience, God allowed me to witness the positive results of my actions in a very public and shocking way.

Obviously I'd like to think my messages to the 2005–06 Greece Athena squad would have sunk in even if J-Mac hadn't ever experienced his big night—but he did. Jason's twenty-point night was a stunning statement about the value of teamwork and displaying true compassion for all kinds of people. Every player on that team demonstrated enormous integrity, which is such an important quality in the lessons I try to teach.

There were all kinds of twists and turns during the 2005–06 season, but in looking back, I'd like to think God rewarded me for being consistent on some important ideals that can apply to all aspects of life, basketball or otherwise. I've developed a list of those points; they serve as the backbone of this book. Although I also enjoy reading books by well-known coaches, motivational experts, and personal-success gurus, the conclusions I've drawn come chiefly from my own life experiences:

Define your passion. There's a reason children are asked, "What do you want to be when you grow up?" It's never too early to start identifying how you might stoke your passions into a lifetime of fulfillment. If you follow what you love, good things will naturally happen. The number one passion for Jason and me is basketball; that's what gives us that extra energy that just seems to make life worth living.

Because J-Mac wears his heart on his sleeve, his saga is enhanced by leaps and bounds. The public was captivated by his obvious enthusiasm during his big game, on the night of the sectional finals, and all through his media appearances. I recognize that outward enthusiasm does not fit all personalities, but a fire does need to be burning somewhere within everybody. Enthusiasm and passion are contagious, and I think this story provided plenty of shots of adrenaline for people around the world who really needed it.

Define your mission. Coaching, for me, is not just about being involved in the sport of basketball. It's about guiding young men into adulthood as well. I also accomplish that mission as a full-time physical education instructor, and what often gets overlooked among scholastic coaches is that many of them are teachers too. The teaching component is much less likely to land you in the newspaper, but I'd say coaching and teaching go hand in hand in a lot of ways because the mission is the same: breeding success in young people.

Doing the right thing is at the forefront for me and my fellow youth coaches—boys' coaches and girls' coaches, from Biddy Basketball to the varsity level, from football to swimming to tennis. Speaking for the great majority of my peers, we care about our athletes first and foremost in the game of life, not from checking the stat sheets. Only a relatively low percentage of my brethren at the scholastic level will ever end up on the national news; they're simply trying to be caring human beings day in and day out. There are a lot more coaches in the business these days for the right reasons than the wrong ones.

J-Mac, meanwhile, carried out his mission as the best basketball manager possible, and to him that took greater priority than whether he got to play. For Jason to accept being manager at the beginning of every season after trying so hard to make the team and coming up short, that took incredible heart. For him to go back to that role after becoming a superstar, that took even more heart.

Set goals. People have asked me after the 2005–06 season, "How do you keep moving forward as a coach? How can you top all these amazing things that happened?" The key is to seek ways of going from good to great. As women's soccer superstar Mia Hamm put it, "Celebrate what you have accomplished, but raise the bar a little higher each time you succeed."

After the night of February 15, I saw that there was so much possible. So I continued to raise my standards. For instance, one of my goals is to win a state championship now. Some would say that's just a pipe dream, and of course the odds are long, but the more positive my attitude the more likely I'll be to reach this goal. In fact, I always maintain a couple of seemingly impossible goals like that. You shouldn't avoid setting goals simply because you live in fear of not reaching them. Besides, you might just find along the way that you're more capable of attaining the so-called impossible dreams than you'd thought.

I have a practice of recording my goals on paper, and it's amazing how powerful a motivator that can be. Whereas goals that are just kept in your mind can be more conveniently dismissed, there's something about the printed word that makes you hesitate to cross them out or crumple that paper up. Another ritual I've adopted is writing a list of twelve to fifteen goals on index cards and reading them out loud in front of a mirror three times a day. These goals range from basketball and career success to being a loving and caring person toward my family, team, and community.

When Lou Holtz lost his job as an assistant football coach at the University of South Carolina many years ago, he sat down and set 107 personal goals that involved all aspects of his life. That almost seems over the top, until you consider that over the years Coach Holtz has achieved all but a handful of them while becoming one of the most respected college coaches ever.

Persevere. Jason is such a great example of somebody who had a dream and kept working for it. How much of his perseverance was due to his autism and the intense focus on certain subjects that is one of the condition's main characteristics? I'm sure that factored into everything, but there was much more going on inside that young man. To think otherwise would be selling his desire and determination way short. I feel that J-Mac accessed something way down inside his soul.

I think the people who have success are those who know how to deal with the roadblocks in life. Do they throw in the towel, or do they figure out how to make a detour and achieve something positive out of a challenging situation? I'd like to encourage others to tap into their reservoir of perseverance. It's something we all have. Personally, I had to persevere mightily after my inaugural varsity season, which produced only one win and a subsequent dismissal from my position. None of that looks good on a young coach's résumé, and for all I know, that could have been the end of my career. But Bill Van Gundy took me under his wing as an assistant at Genesee Community College, and I soon got back into the varsity ranks and never looked back.

Fast-forward to the 2005–06 season. Just a couple of weeks in, I was looking to resign. But I've always emphasized the value of perseverance, and that point was reiterated often by the many people who thought I should stick it out. Without actually saying it, they were telling me not to be a hypocrite. That was a humbling experience, being reminded to live by the very words that I preach.

Carpe diem. No better model for seizing the day exists than my man J-Mac. His big opportunity finally arrived on February 15, and he was ready because he had stayed true to his passion, his mission, his goals, and his sense of perseverance. He wasn't just given an opportunity, but in a sense he created it. I didn't give J-Mac a chance to play out of pity. I did it because he was an exceptionally dedicated team manager who had totally earned his reward. To seize the day, you have to have an outstanding work ethic and a positive attitude. J-Mac has both. I always preach to my players that to be great you must be exceptional in things you can control, and you can control your work ethic and attitude. There is no substitute for hard work and a positive attitude.

There's one more point of reflection regarding carpe diem. Would you rather seize the day, or let the day seize you? If you come across a dream job opening and there are three hundred candidates for that position, will you attempt to stand out from the pack or just assume you don't stand a chance? If you want to ask somebody you're really attracted to on a date, will you take that leap of faith or retreat into a shell? Yes, there is the possibility of rejection, failure, embarrassing moments, you name it. But I really believe you improve the odds of getting what you want out of life by seizing the day. Don't count on these important things being handed to you. Fantasy worlds aren't going to work. Making your dreams come true comes back to taking action and not being passive.

Be a team player. Jason's shooting barrage was so extraordinary, it stood to overshadow everything else that was captured on tape. But another major component of those magical few minutes was how the other Athena players got the ball to J-Mac incessantly. They wanted to give their special teammate every chance to shine, even though nobody had told them ahead of time to pass off like that.

Many more examples of being a team player were evident on that night. Jason's teammates on the bench went wild every time he scored a basket; they were so happy for him. A few hours before the game began, Matt Sheehan was down with an injury and Steve Kerr wanted to wear his uniform. This was a group with some amazing character. You don't go through the kind of turmoil we did and still win a league co-championship and sectionals without a real sense of team.

Then there's Jason himself. He accepted going back to being a manager after his twenty-point night because it was more important for him to see Athena win sectionals than to get to play again. He not only returned willingly to his normal role; he embraced it and didn't lose an ounce of enthusiasm.

Stay true to yourself. Jason has retained his innocence despite his ascent to stardom, and that's only served to enhance his appeal. I've never heard him say a bad word about anybody, either before or after he became a national media darling. Jason has lived his celebrity with such class. That says a lot about what he's like on the inside. I think the most likable and respected athletes and movie stars are those who can conduct themselves in a similar fashion, never getting too caught up in their celebrity—people like Magic Johnson, who never seems to stop smiling, or Cal Ripken Jr., who's been a great role model both on the field and off.

As for me, I like to keep the expression "EGO stands for Edging God Out" in the forefront of my mind. One time a lady sitting next to me on an airplane asked how the publicity surrounding the J-Mac story has changed my life, and I said not one bit regarding my basic personality. As much as this experience has made me a lot busier, I really don't feel I've changed as a person. Integrity is very important to me and I want to treat people right. Besides, you need to stay humble because in coaching, the lows can be right around the corner from the highs.

Actually, your real character tends to surface when things *aren't* going your way. My biggest gut-check along those lines was going through all those sleepless nights early in the 2005–06 season. Had I quit my coaching job, I would have relieved myself of considerable stress but not been true to my mission of being a leader.

Share your success. As coach of a varsity sports team, I recognize that we have high visibility within the community and therefore we should use that status to give back. One of the most touching letters I got in 2006 was from Joan and Bill Reeves, who recalled that while I was coaching at Greece Olympia, our team organized a benefit car wash in 1995 in honor of their daughter Stephanie, an Olympia student who died of cancer.

The J-Mac story is one that I truly believe needs to be kept alive, not because it brought us celebrity status but because there is so much lasting importance riding on it. If the goodness that came out of Greece Athena High School on that winter night in 2006 can help put autism more in the public eye, then I feel I have the responsibility to get behind that any way I can. Thus, many of my public speaking appearances are to special-needs groups.

Jason, obviously, has been a giant in terms of autism awareness, and he and his family accepted this responsibility from the get-go even though they had no real chance to prepare for it. J-Mac continues to be an excellent spokesperson by appearing at banquets and other special events. I think I speak for both of us when I say we want to give hope to anybody trying to overcome adversity, whether it's autism or something else. In talking to different speakers' bureaus, I was asked what my target audience is and I replied that mine is somewhat universal because this story touches everyone—parents, grandparents, kids.

Along with all the above points that I've laid out, I'd like to implore folks to **believe in miracles.** *Miracle* is a word that's come up often in the correspondence I've received regarding February 15, and I'm in full agreement that a miracle is what we experienced.

Why us? How did an autistic team manager and his high school coach end up being the center of such an amazing experience? I look at it from a faith perspective. Over and over, Gospel accounts of miracles performed by Jesus involve everyday folks. Some of them had disabilities and illness. All had faith, and they became a positive example for others. As it turned out, I'd say J-Mac and I were just the kind of people God might employ to send a message of hope to the rest of the world in the form of a timeless feel-good story.

I also believe God meant for J-Mac to score so many points just so the performance would get into that rarefied air of a sports miracle and create maximum impact. Think about it: For all the great sporting events that have taken place over the years, only a very few have earned miracle status. One was the 1969 New York Mets victory in the World Series, which earned them the title Miracle Mets. Only seven years prior to that, the Mets were an expansion franchise that had set new lows in ineptitude, posting a 40-120 record in their first year. They then finished in last or next-to-last place every season until 1969, when they won the National League pennant before shocking the heavily favored Baltimore Orioles in the World Series.

Then came the 1980 Miracle on Ice. I don't think we'll ever get enough of Al Michaels's cries of "Do you believe in miracles? Yes!" in the final seconds of the United States hockey team's epic 4-3 upset of the USSR. This was a bunch of college and amateur hockey players knocking off the best team in the world, and two days later the US went on to win the Olympic gold medal by beating Finland 4-2.

How does J-Mac's feat compare? Well, first of all we have the New York connection going: The Mets clinched the World Series at Shea Stadium in New York City, and the US hockey team captured its gold medal upstate from Rochester in Lake Placid. All three stories involve an individual or team that rose from relative obscurity.

With both the Miracle Mets and the Miracle on Ice, victories were earned against seemingly invincible opponents. I believe J-Mac fits right into this category as well. The giant he overcame was his disability, and he did that in truly miraculous fashion.

So many other things happened within our team as part of the miracle. How about Kourtney Goff being the first to greet Jason at game's end, after he and his brother had endured so much discomfort during the season because of the drama involving their father dropping out as assistant coach? How about Steve Kerr, who used to be rather immature in my opinion, taking J-Mac under his wing as well as the entire special-education program at Greece Athena, where he ended up volunteering considerable time? How about Terrance McCutchen, who struggled over a lack of playing time during the season but still did all he could to make Jason shine on February 15, rather than be concerned about himself?

It's also miraculous that we have these precious moments preserved on video. A couple of parents' camcorders picked up a lot of the action, but nobody really nailed it like Marcus Luciano, a student who had virtually no experience with videography. Without his presence of mind to capture this evidence, I really don't know how many people would have believed the miracle ever happened.

Then there was the matter of my sectional title drought. Seventeen days after Jason's big game I earned my first sectional championship as a head coach, after many years of agonizing over how I kept coming so close but falling short each time. God works in funny ways.

There's more, lots more. What's been really interesting to me is that during Jason's celebrity rounds he met so many people who ended up winning championships as well. We were guests at the University of Florida's team dinner at the NCAA Final Four, and then the Gators went on to the win the NCAA title. J-Mac became manager that spring of our local professional basketball team, the Rochester RazorSharks, and they won the league championship. We met Peyton Manning at the Rochester Press-Radio Club dinner that spring, and Jason worked for his Indianapolis Colts at their summer camp. Voilà, Indy won its first Super Bowl the following February. We were guests at a benefit dinner hosted by Robert Horry, of the San Antonio Spurs, in the summer of 2006, and his club captured the NBA title the next spring. I simply call it the power of J-Mac, and for all I know it's all connected to the miracle.

Will another autistic child go on a scoring rampage like J-Mac? It seems unlikely. But even if a few more kids with disabilities make one bucket, or get a bit of playing time, or are included in some other way, these are all steps forward. Miracles are meant to inspire, to bring about positive change in people who were touched by the miracle. Look at all the extra awareness that's been placed on autism, raising the likelihood of additional funding toward research and increasing the possibility of autistic people being accepted into the mainstream. Think of all the parents of special-needs children who have been given renewed hope.

"It sends out the message that people with autism have real abilities and skills. They may be good at one thing and not at another, but they can take the thing they're good at and build on it and broaden it out. Autistic people always keep learning, always keep learning," said Temple Grandin.

One of the biggest calls for the inclusion of people with special needs came about through Special Olympics International, which developed in the late 1960s through the efforts of the Kennedy family and now serves more than three million athletes in 150 countries. Dr. Timothy Shriver—the current Special Olympics chairperson, whose parents, Eunice Kennedy Shriver (sister of John F. and Robert F. Kennedy) and Robert Sargent Shriver Jr., were the founders of Special Olympics—agreed with Ms. Grandin about the importance of this miracle. "I think it's a tremendous accomplishment and a great lesson, a reminder that a community needs to give these people all the opportunities it can. It doesn't matter whether your IQ is twenty or two hundred," Dr. Shriver said. "Everybody has a gift inside of them, and it's up to the community to unlock that gift."

Nationally renowned sportswriter Mike Lupica, who has a longtime association with Special Olympics in his home state of Connecticut, noted that the scene on February 15 was "a pure form of the joy of sports, the way you see with the athletes of Special Olympics. The joy of just participating, then the joy of doing something extraordinary. That's what I saw with Jason: him doing what we all want to do, in and out of sports, which means finding the very best of himself."

The fact that the miracle occurred during a sporting event is vital to the CBS Final Four broadcasting duo of Jim Nantz and Billy Packer: "Heroic, that's what we all see in Jason," Jim said. "Sports sometimes can identify heroes and create these most unlikely scripts. There's no other walk of life that can bring that, that can hit home to so many people."

"Regardless of who you were rooting for, you got caught up in the moment," Billy added, noting that sports has the power to unite or divide humans and "this was like a unifying event."

"The events are a case study in why sports moves people. What people saw that night was unity that is hard to find," added Tom Rinaldi, who did a couple of wonderful features on us for ESPN. "So much in American life divides us, and oftentimes we are only united in adversity or tragedy. Isn't it fantastic that here was a moment that united people in joy and in admiration?"

The patriotic aspects of this saga were echoed by former New York governor George Pataki. "First, the fact the coach made the decision and second, not just the players but the entire crowd was rooting for J-Mac—it just brings out the best in our country when the underdog is given an opportunity and rises up," Governor Pataki said. "The United States has always been a country where you rooted for the underdog. This gives us all occasion to smile, feel good, and say, 'Hey, yes, this is a great country.'"

When I watch TV news and read the newspaper, it seems that ninety percent of the stories are negative—this person got murdered, that one got robbed, Sept. 11, Hurricane Katrina, car crashes, stock market woes, conflict in Afghanistan and Iraq. So much negativity, so much tragedy and sadness. Every day is a life-and-death struggle for many who face challenges far greater than anything on my plate or Jason McElwain's.

You turn to the sports page to get away from that, and even there you might find blaring headlines about steroid investigations, sex scandals involving athletes and coaches, NCAA violations, salary disputes concerning mega-millionaire athletes. Then our story comes along. To this day, people approach me to say that it was just so good to see a positive story.

"Let's face it, there's just so much tragic stuff to report on, so much negativity that just pulls us down. We get tired of it; it makes you wonder if the end of the world is coming," remarked Scott Pitoniak, our local columnist.

Scott said he also appreciated how our saga is abundant with true happiness and emotion, as opposed to the endless parade of reality shows and their manufactured tears on cue. "I just think it resonated with so many people because it's not contrived. This was not planned; it was pure, unadulterated joy. Reality shows are not reality; they're misnomers. This is a real story."

> **You can live a lifetime and never come across a story like that. It's one of my favorite stories and one of my favorite clips—as they say, "the feel-good story of the year." I still get choked up when I think about what Jim did, putting Jason in the game.**
>
> —Steve Hartman, *CBS Evening News*

I occasionally flip on old news features of the miracle night. Many people who wrote to me noted how they've played the video over and over—a nice break in the day, especially when you've had a rough one. I still struggle to view these tapes and DVDs without becoming at least a little teary-eyed. In fact, as many times as I've told this story in interviews and public presentations, it's still not unusual for me to get choked up. People say they enjoy my speeches because I speak from my heart. I can't imagine that I'll ever get tired of sharing something this powerful. It leaves me with such a good, warm feeling.

Has the event made all the problems in my life disappear? Of course not. But it does serve as a personal reminder of the power of perseverance, and how that increases the odds of getting through the tough times. I'd like to also think that I've always believed in miracles, and if I hadn't, perhaps the events of February 15 wouldn't have unfolded. I may not have been coaching anymore. I may not have won a sectional title.

I've been gratified to discover how many other people believe in miracles too. The thing that keeps getting spelled out by people who write and come up to me is, "You've given us hope." I think God wanted to create a story of hope for our whole world to share in, a reminder that there are still some neat things going on. Regardless of your religious persuasion, the fact is that when faith and hope are alive, miracles can occur.

I believe that's why God put me on this earth, to spread that message of faith and hope. Forty-six years later, I got to experience that part of God's plan for me. I made a decision that ended up changing Jason's life and inspiring a lot of other people as a result, and you know what? It was never intended that way. It was simply, in my heart, the right thing to do.

Jason, too, has an innate sense of keeping his priorities straight. In the end, one might have assumed that his top thrill was scoring twenty points in a game. But to this day, J-Mac will tell anybody who wishes to listen that being part of a championship team was better. From the day he became our manager, through all our team turmoil in 2005–06, to the February day that season when I handed him a uniform for the first time, he was Greece Athena basketball's biggest fan.

As for me, I had always thought that capturing a sectional title would be my own top thrill in coaching. Instead, the events of February 15, 2006, rank higher.

That's when, in helping somebody's dream come true, I saw a miracle unfold right before my eyes. Seek to do the same in your own life, and you just might end up experiencing a miracle yourself.

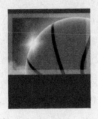

Epilogue

THE POSITIVE VIBES FROM 2005–06 CARRIED RIGHT over into the following season. After waiting so long for my first sectional title, it took only a year for the process to repeat itself.

Our top six guys in 2006–07 were all varsity veterans from the miracle year—Terrance McCutchen, Rob Zappia, Brian Benson, Kourtney Goff, Kyle Boline, and Matt Davies. We got a good taste of tough competition during a December tournament in Florida and I was pleased that we won two of our four games. The experience humbled us but also made us aware that we had some potential.

We won the league title, dropping only one division game that year. It was probably my best defensive team ever, which was evident in our sectional championship win over McQuaid Jesuit, which ended with a score of 39-36. They almost had to bring the peach baskets back out for that one. Just before the title game we were graced by locker room pep talks from two major cogs of the previous year's team: Steve Kerr and J-Mac. Jason kept it real simple, telling the guys it was a special night and to stay focused. We did stay focused enough to earn our second straight sectional, which had never before happened at Greece Athena, even during the John Wallace era of the early 1990s.

The following year, in 2007–08, I felt that I had one of my most talented squads ever. We went undefeated in the league but were stopped in the sectional semifinals. Not long after the season ended, our center, Brian Benson—one of the guys who went out of his way to pass to J-Mac during his historic game, and who had blossomed into quite a player—signed a full Division I scholarship with the University of New Hampshire.

One nice spring afternoon in May 2008, I walked into my office at Greece Athena and who was there but J-Mac, now nineteen years old, chatting away with a couple of my colleagues as he waited for me. I had seen him around sporadically after his senior year, particularly since Greece Athena is right next to the YMCA on Long Pond Road and Jason is over there all the time playing pickup games. We also went on the occasional public speaking engagement together. But on this particular day, J-Mac had something in mind that involved the resurrection of a more permanent relationship.

He said, "Coach, I've got an idea I want to talk to you about. Is there any way I can come back and be part of the program? I really miss it." He thought that since I already had a few assistants, perhaps he could work on a volunteer basis with the junior varsity under Mike Setzer, who has always maintained a special relationship with him. I told him, "Yeah, J-Mac, I think that would be a real good idea." I was thrilled to have him back in the fold.

So Jason began coming to summer leagues and started to get really involved again. Beginning in the fall of 2008, he faithfully attended the JV practices and also sat on the bench for all the JV and varsity games. He even had business cards printed up that listed him as a program assistant for Greece Athena basketball. You've got to love that.

As it turned out, the power of J-Mac was as potent as ever in 2008–09. First we tied for the league championship, our fourth straight year of either winning or tying for it. From there, we were down by fifteen or sixteen points to East High in the second half of our sectional semifinal and came back to win. We also trailed Irondequoit by double digits in the title game, but rallied for a narrow victory to claim our third sectional crown in four tries. It had been three years since Jason had served as team manager for that breakthrough sectional title—which was also won against Irondequoit—and here he was all over again, celebrating on the Blue Cross Arena floor.

As if making two straight second-half comebacks with our season on the line wasn't enough, we outdid ourselves in the state qualifier against Gates Chili. With less than a minute to go in the third quarter, we were down by twenty points, and a blowout loss was right around the corner. We somehow managed to send the game into overtime and win; it was easily the greatest comeback I've ever been associated with as a coach. That put us in the state quarterfinals and although we bowed out at that point, it was the furthest a team of mine had ever advanced. This all happened in J-Mac's first year back with the program, and somehow I wasn't surprised. Whenever improbable things occur and J-Mac is nearby, it just seems like an extension of that miracle from 2006.

In 2009–10 our string of four straight league titles or co-titles was snapped, as we finished second in Monroe County Division II and reached the Section 5 semifinals. Jason carried on predominantly in the same role as the previous season, working with small groups of JV players during practice and yelling encouragement from the sidelines during games. He also talked to players individually and tried to get them pumped up. When people see him on the sidelines these days, they may well recognize his distinctive face with the large lips and innocent expression, but no longer does he resemble the diminutive five-foot-seven-inch team manager they once knew. Due to a delayed growth spurt, he is now about six feet tall.

Sometimes my players haven't known how to initially react to Jason because of his disability, and that's no different than before. For instance, his voice is naturally loud, which can be disconcerting if you think he's chewing you out all the time. And, of course, he repeats his pet expressions, like "stay focused," over and over. But players eventually see how great his passion and desire for the program is, and they ultimately can't help but love him. He just bleeds Athena Trojan black and gold, and his dedication remains highly infectious.

Heading into 2010–11 I've devised a new role for Jason, a promotion of sorts, as a varsity assistant. This involves his attendance at all the varsity practices, and I know he's very reliable, having missed only a handful of practices with the JVs over two seasons.

J-Mac has certainly been a welcome presence, simply by the fact that he was a pivotal figure when Greece Athena basketball hit a new level of success in 2005–06. I'm happy to see that our upward ascent has continued, and there's no question that kids coming into the program have fed off J-Mac's miracle. Of course, I've also been blessed with superbly talented teams, and these players have worked hard for everything they've gotten. Put it all together, and each year brings a group of guys who are motivated by carrying on this excellence and who expect to compete for championships. In fact, for the 2008–09 season we borrowed from Jim Tressel, the Ohio State football coach, in developing our slogan, With Tradition Comes Responsibility. In other words, tradition doesn't graduate. New players must acquire a sense of ownership to carry on what was begun.

A little aside: During 2008–09 Nancy Kalb, the mom of one of my top players, R. J. Kalb, told me that during the holidays she just didn't feel like making cookies as she had for many years previously. Just after she had decided not to do it, she saw our slogan somewhere in her house—and she started right in on those cookies.

As our basketball program has continued its immense success, the J-Mac story has exhibited remarkable staying power. Anybody unfamiliar with it can get a taste simply by punching "J-Mac" into a search engine, and all kinds of news reports and features from 2006, along with game video, are bound to pop up.

I realize that even the most popular of stories begin to take a backseat in the public domain after a certain amount of time has passed, but this one keeps surfacing in some form or another. J-Mac is still sought after for national interviews, with reports being most plentiful around the anniversary of his twenty-point game. He is still a featured guest at banquets and makes other special appearances, and every summer, thanks to the friendship he struck up with Peyton Manning, he attends the Indianapolis Colts training camp as a volunteer equipment manager.

In August 2007 Jason was part of a "where are they now" segment on NBC's *Today Show,* and he was shown at his part-time supermarket bakery job, waving at the camera. In June 2008 Tom Coughlin, head coach of the New York Giants and a native of the Rochester area, referenced J-Mac when he appeared as a guest at the Rochester Press-Radio Club dinner shortly after his team's epic upset of the New England Patriots in Super Bowl XLIV. Coach Coughlin noted that he had once shown the tape of J-Mac's game in training camp, and that you could hear a pin drop.

Also in 2008, a local elderly man on his deathbed asked to meet Jason because he was so inspired by him. J-Mac willingly and graciously honored that very special request. During the 2009 Super Bowl, Jason was featured in a debut TV ad for Gatorade that also included the likes of Michael Jordan, Mia Hamm, John Wooden, Peyton Manning, and Billie Jean King.

In the late winter of 2010 I sent a note of congratulations to Steve Donahue, head coach of Cornell University, when the Big Red clinched an NCAA tournament bid by winning the Ivy League title. Steve had first established contact with me back in 2006, writing a nice letter following J-Mac's big game and noting that he has an autistic son. After receiving my congratulatory letter, he e-mailed me with an invitation to the Big Red's Selection Sunday party. J-Mac and I went over to Ithaca and had a really good experience. Steve gave J-Mac his phone number and they called each other a few times; that developed into a national story because Steve was in the news quite a bit during that period. The Big Red became the first Ivy League team in thirty-one years to reach the NCAA Sweet 16, and this success landed Steve a coveted new job as head coach at Boston College in the Atlantic Coast Conference.

It's great to have ongoing recognition, and both Jason and I look forward to a renewed jolt of public interest in our story when the movie on Jason's life—in which my character plays a significant role—comes out. The movie remains in development by Columbia Pictures.

Yet day in and day out, what's most important for Jason and his family is that he has stability. He gets that by living at home and logging four mornings per week in the bakery department of Wegmans, the grocery store where he has worked since high school. He also puts in an occasional weekend night busing tables at the Brook House, a popular Italian restaurant in Greece.

J-Mac continues to be the consummate sports nut. He loves calling up his Athena basketball-playing friends to meet him over at the Y for some hoops. He has developed nice bonds with so many of them, especially those from the 2005–06 team. He calls me almost every day to talk about something related to Athena basketball, and he gets a kick out of buzzing up local radio sports talk shows to put in his two cents' worth.

Since he rejoined Athena basketball, Jason has also become a volunteer assistant with our high school's freshman football and modified baseball programs. I feel these roles are key, since he didn't go on to college or get his driver's license. For all that he has accomplished, there are still certain limitations involved with having autism and a learning disability. We've continued to work hard with J-Mac on keeping his emotions under control during games, which at times can be very difficult for him. Due in part to the disability, he has never been able to accept losing very well and wears his heart on his sleeve. But now that he's a coach, we've stressed the importance of him setting an example, and he's made a lot of progress.

Coaching has undoubtedly become J-Mac's next passion, and his involvement is just as vital for him today as it was when he first became a JV basketball team manager under Jeff Amoroso. Jason is a happy young man and I can see him staying in the roles he currently holds for a very long time. I'm so proud that Jason has remained true to those intangibles I constantly preach about: defining your passion, goals, and mission; putting the team before the individual; being true to yourself; and so forth.

As for me, I still do the occasional media interview in relation to J-Mac, but what has really gained momentum is my public speaking. I use the J-Mac story as my foundation for motivational talks about making dreams come true and believing in God's miracles, and am very pleased that I've received a number of standing ovations. Speaking has really become my passion, as I average ten engagements per year with organizations and companies across the country. I look forward to making a transition into full-time speaking after retirement from teaching in a few years.

I've also created my own website, CoachJimJohnson.com, and this whole experience has been lots of fun, opening up some doors and allowing me to meet all kinds of people.

A Coach and a Miracle

I turned fifty years old in 2009 and life is great. I'm approaching thirty years in the Greece school district, and coaching remains just as much a passion for me as ever. In 2007 Pat and I celebrated our twenty-fifth wedding anniversary, and in the spring of 2010 Tyler, our only child, completed his freshman year as a criminology major at the University of Maryland; he plans to attend law school.

With Tyler now attending college out of state, it's very touching for me to have J-Mac back in the mix at Athena. In many respects he is like a son to me, and everyone connected with Trojan basketball is like a second family to both of us. It's awesome to continue my bond with this autistic young man who—through what seemed like a rather obscure coaching gesture on my part in 2006—ended up starring in one of the most universally captivating feel-good stories of our time.

Jim Johnson
November 2010

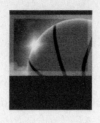

Acknowledgements

THERE AREN'T NEARLY ENOUGH PAGES AVAILABLE to thank everybody who contributed in some way to this book. Among the folks who deserve special mention:

My co-author and longtime friend, Mike Latona, for his excellent writing skills and ability to dig details out of me with his insights and probing questions;

Matthew Kelly, publisher of Beacon Publishing, for believing in our project;

My wife, Pat, and son, Tyler for their unbelievable love, support and commitment as I've pursued my teaching/coaching career and now this book venture;

My parents, Gene and Rita, for their unwavering love through thick and thin and for still faithfully attending my Greece Athena games;

My siblings Tom, Mark, Julie, Kathy and Danny, with special thanks to Tom for his wise advice on my business dealings past and present;

Jason "J-Mac" McElwain, for his perseverance and passion for the game of basketball, in particular his ongoing love for Greece Athena hoops;

Jason's parents, Dave and Debbie, and brother, Josh, for the many ways that they've supported Athena basketball;

Andy McCormack, J-Mac's speech/language pathologist, for his friendship with Jason as well as making the first call to a TV station after his big scoring night;

Mike Setzer, my junior varsity coach, a terrific coach and more importantly an outstanding friend to both Jason and me;

Jeff Amoroso, my former JV coach, who gave Jason his first shot as a basketball manager and therefore deserves the credit for all that followed;

Greece Athena basketball coaches Justin Mull, Don Brown and Kevin Damann;

All my players past and present, especially the 2005-06 title team with special thanks to Rickey Wallace and Terrance McCutchen for sharing their insights for this book;

The administration of Greece Central School District and Greece Athena High School, especially secretary Ann Marie Paul and former athletic director Randy Hutto;

Kelvin Goff, my former volunteer assistant coach, who put in tremendous time and effort for six years;

Rob Cerone, Stan Cipura and Mike Butler, my office buddies at Athena, and Jason Bunting, our public-address announcer;

Jay Shelofsky, our unofficial photographer, and Marcus Luciano, our student videographer on the night of Feb. 15, 2006;

Cheryl Tisa, our scorekeeper who has also made big behind-the-scenes contributions;

My players' parents for their endless volunteer time, particularly Rick and Nancy Kalb;

Chris Cardon, Troy Prince, Steve DeRooy, Roger Klimek, Doug Childs and my other cohorts in the coaching fraternity;

Josh Harter, John Pelin and all the 2005-06 Spencerport players for their amazing displays of sportsmanship;

Rick Admundson, Dave Richardson, Phil Abel and my other associates throughout the Monroe County League and Section 5;

Celebrity coaches, media, politicians and others who willingly gave their time to be interviewed for this book, starting with Billy Donovan, a real class act who wrote the foreword. Also, alphabetically: Dan Arruda, Jim Baron, Jim Boeheim, John Calipari, Mike Catalana, Seth Davis, Temple Grandin, Steve Hartman, Paul Hewitt, Jim Larranaga, Mike Lupica, Jack McKinney, Jim Nantz, Billy Packer, Gov. George Pataki, Scott Pitoniak, Sarah Rinaldi, Tom Rinaldi, Sen. Joseph Robach, Dr. Timothy P. Shriver, Bill Van Gundy, Jeff Van Gundy, Dick Vitale, John Wallace, Reggie Witherspoon and Jay Wright;

Pat Williams of the Orlando Magic for his guidance in our book-publishing process;

Frank Scatoni of Venture Literary Agency, for his input in shaping this book early on;

All the Rochester-area media who have covered Greece Athena over the years, with a special thank-you to my friend Scott Pitoniak for sharing his book-writing wisdom;

My national speaking bureaus, especially Phillip Van Hooser, former president of the National Speakers Association;

Fred Garwood for his friendship and excellent legal advice;

And all the folks who reached out through phone calls, e-mails and letters to share their appreciation of the miracle I experienced, with an extra-big thanks to those connected with the special-needs population.

Finally, I thank God for selecting me to be a part of this miracle.

About the Co-Author

Mike Latona is the senior staff writer for the *Catholic Courier* newspaper in Rochester, where he has earned five individual first-place national awards and numerous staff honors over two decades in the Catholic press. He also contributes to national Catholic magazines and is a former youth minister in the Diocese of Rochester. Mike is a graduate of Syracuse University. He resides in Greece with his wife, Paola; sons, Andrew and Matthew; and daughter, Catherine.

A Note From the Co-Author

Life sure works in funny ways.

I've known Jim Johnson since the mid-1970s, when I kept the scorebook while he was a sharp-shooting guard for Greece Arcadia High School. We've reconnected many times throughout his coaching and my journalism career, maintaining a bond and mutual trust that can only exist between people whose association dates back to childhood. Still, I couldn't have imagined that we'd someday be writing a book together.

In early 2006 when Coach Johnson and Jason McElwain burst into the national spotlight, I was captivated for two reasons: my link with Jim and also with autism. The timing of this story was profound because within the previous few months, not one but both of my sons—Andrew, then 4 years old, and Matthew, then 2—were diagnosed as falling on the autism spectrum.

It gave me great hope to hear of an autistic child finding success with Jim's support. That spring, a proud moment occurred when Jason shook my boys' hands during a chance meeting at the YMCA in Greece.

Needless to say, I've been moved in a special way by sharing Jim's story while dealing with the many highs and lows of autism right under my own roof. I owe many thanks to Jim for extending me this opportunity and it has been a real labor of love. We've had an absolute blast working together.

In addition to the folks Coach Johnson has already mentioned, I'd like to acknowledge the number one people in my life: my loving wife, Paola, who has backed me in every aspect of this project; and my awesome children Andrew, Matthew and Catherine. Special thanks to my dad, Pat, and late mother, Ruth. I am nothing without all they have given me in my life. Thanks also to my sibs Jean, Mary Jo, Julie and Tom, and the rest of my terrific family.

A very special thank-you to John Rosengren for his tremendous feedback any time I needed it. Thanks also to Kate Rickard Williams for her numerous efforts on my behalf.

I appreciate the steady encouragement provided by the administration and staff at the *Catholic Courier* and Diocese of Rochester. Further thanks go out to many friends and acquaintances in the media world who have helped in some way bring this book to fruition, with special kudos to Beth Dotson Brown, Kevin Burns, Mary DeMarle, Peter Lovenheim, Maria Ruiz Scaperlanda, Carrie Swearingen and Peter Wallin.

I thank Nancy Sharp, my newspaper professor at Syracuse University, whose personal interest in my future helped bring about the eventual realization that I was meant to be a writer.

And thank you, God, for sticking close by every moment of my life.

—Mike Latona

Coach Jim Johnson offers
the following services and products.

✸ Keynote speeches:

Dreams Really Do Come True

Leadership That Makes Your Dreams Come True

Teamwork That Makes Dreams Come True

✸ Workshops:

Leadership (90-minute and half-day),

Personal Development (90-minute and half-day)

✸ Motivational DVD:

Two Games That Demonstrate the Essence of Perseverance

For more information, visit www.coachjimjohnson.com